# Floppy Ears
### and
# Puppy Dog Tales

# Get Your Free Gift!

To get the best experience with this book, I've found readers who download and use the free journal are able to implement the steps easier and get the most from the questions asked that lead to the next steps in the process of healing.

You can get a copy by visiting:
**https://dl.bookfunnel.com/xtm1s0imnt**

*"I really didn't realize I had gone through all the chapters, as the book compelled me to continue reading, as if I were stuffing popcorn in my mouth while watching an intense movie and then reaching in the bowl, not looking only to feel the unwanted kernels, and then the book was complete!"*

*~Tena Clark~*

*"Ms. Moran, a certified drug and alcohol and domestic violence counselor, has helped numerous individuals and families deal with loss and grief. When her beloved Irish terrier, Paddy, her companion of fifteen years, died, it sent her into a deep depression, one from which she wasn't sure she could recover. To overcome this tremendous pain, she drew from her experiences and began journaling her memories of her own grief and time spent with her favorite companion. What she learned during this process saved her life. Afterward, she felt a compelling need to share this knowledge with others and decided to write this book with the ultimate goal of helping others suffering their own loss. Ms. Moran's testimony is a blueprint to help understand the stages of grief and eventually bring joy back to life. It is well-written, honest, and heartfelt. Anyone needing a helping hand to overcome loss will definitely benefit from reading this book."* Doc Macomber is an award-winning author. His latest book is Little Tiger.

*~Doc Macomber~*

"If you have ever loved another, whether pet or person, then this book is a must-read. There's no jargon, yet it puts the most difficult emotions to words in a straightforward, easy-to-read, and relatable fashion. It feels like a conversation with a friend, which is invaluable when you're grieving.

Even if you're not currently grieving, this book can aid you in examining your relationships and the lessons to be learned from them. It can also help you empathize with those who are grieving and support them better on their journey.

This book may be targeted toward pet owners, but it's so much more than that. It's a wonderful guide on the importance of appreciating those we love, grieving the ones who are gone, and learning from everyone around us - including our pets."

*~Zac Moran~*

"I didn't think this book would affect me as much as it did! Here it is a month or so after reading it and I have realized how I never gave myself the time to grieve and have stuffed so many things inside. This book has been a reminder to treat myself better, and as I do, fondly remember my losses, my animals, and my loved one., It's ok to feel these feelings and have these memories! I welcome them now!

*~Jennifer Jenkins~*

"Your book helped me realize I don't always appreciate Ginger (my dog) enough. She is our dog, and she likes to keep us company. It also made me realize I rushed through the grief process instead of letting grief transform me into a better person. If you have a dog(s) or are grieving the loss of your dog(s), please read this book. If your dogs are alive, you will appreciate them more. The book also helps in dealing with grief. It shows you what it looks like in its various stages, and guides you through the grief process so you can be transformed as a result of allowing yourself time to deal with grief."

~Sarah Mathews~

**When the world around me is going crazy, and I'm losing faith in humanity, I just have to take one look at my dog to know that good still exists.**

**Dogs are love on 4 legs.com**

# Floppy Ears
## and
# Puppy Dog Tales

**How to Overcome Grief from Loss**
and Other Life Lessons I learned from My Pet

# Diana Lee

Copyright © 2024 by Diana Lee Moran
**Floppy Ears and Puppy Dog Tales**

All rights reserved. No part of this publication may be reproduced, distributed, or transmitted in any form or by any means, including photocopying, recording, or other electronic or mechanical methods, without the prior written permission of the publisher, except in the case of brief quotations embodied in critical reviews and certain other noncommercial uses permitted by copyright law.

Although the author and publisher have made every effort to ensure that the information in this book was correct at press time, the author and publisher do not assume and hereby disclaim any liability to any party for any loss, damage, or disruption caused by errors or omissions, whether such errors or omissions result from negligence, accident, or any other cause.

Adherence to all applicable laws and regulations, including international, federal, state, and local governing professional licensing, business practices, advertising, and all other aspects of doing business in the US, Canada or any other jurisdiction is the sole responsibility of the reader and consumer.

Neither the author nor the publisher assumes any responsibility or liability whatsoever on behalf of the consumer or reader of this material. Any perceived slight of any individual or organization is purely unintentional.

The resources in this book are provided for informational purposes only and should not be used to replace the specialized training and professional judgment of a health care or mental health care professional.

Neither the author nor the publisher can be held responsible for the use of the information provided within this book. Please always consult a trained professional before making any decision regarding treatment of yourself or others.

ISBN: 979-8-88759-409-5 - paperback
ISBN: 979-8-88759-410-1 - ebook

# Dedication

This book is dedicated to…

*When the Self Publishing School* advised me to write to just one person, I knew who that person would be. I dedicate this book to my long-time buddy Jan McCarty. If only one person would benefit from my experience and growing knowledge, I would choose her. I know many people here on earth have endured many painful and devastating struggles. However, I have never personally known anyone like my friend who has held their pain so tightly, nor through the whole of their life. I could see the joy she missed while preoccupied with her misery. She has been the first to read my book and expressed how therapeutic it was for her. I pray my book changes her life, and she finds the joy she has long left behind.

I also dedicate this book to all those who have experienced loss and are not living the life they deserve.

*Petey–Jan's doggie*

# Table of Contents

Introduction — 1

Chapter 1 — 7
Expert on grieving?

The Day Paddy Died — 27

Chapter 2 — 35
Pet or Friend?

Chapter 3 — 47
Life After Death

Chapter 4 — 59
Recovery Peace Joy

Chapter 5 — 79
What are Stages of Grief?

Chapter 6 — 89
Stage One—Denial

Chapter 7 — 101
Stage Two—Anger

| | |
|---|---|
| CHAPTER 8<br>Working Through the Grief—Bargaining | 117 |
| CHAPTER 9<br>The Onset of Depression | 135 |
| CHAPTER 10<br>Moving on With Our Lives—Acceptance | 161 |
| CHAPTER 11<br>Finding Meaning in Life Again | 187 |
| CHAPTER 12<br>What I Love About You | 201 |
| CONCLUSION<br>The end is never the ending | 213 |
| ACKNOWLEDGMENTS | 233 |
| INDEX OF QUOTES | 235 |
| INDEX TO THE STAGES OF GRIEF | 241 |
| CHART OF MOODS AND EMOTIONS | 251 |

*Bella—Charlotte Ryan's puppy*

*"Our pets don't live as long as we do because they already know what we humans take so long to learn." ~Diana Lee~*

# INTRODUCTION

I fell into what I thought would be an unrecoverable tailspin when my sixteen-year-old dog died and I cried constantly. I could not complete one mundane task. In response, I wrote about the pain and loss. Journaling helps me handle stress, anxiety, and uncertainties in life. As I began writing every day, I discovered feelings I didn't know I possessed. I could better grasp how I might proceed in living my life within the pain. Additionally, I also realized I had losses in my past I hadn't recognized and grieved over. It is these incomplete grievances that have stunted my relationships and personal growth. As a result, I was not living the most rewarding life possible.

I now understand how much of a friend my dog had been and how he taught me through my different life stages. He helped me be a better friend through his example. He taught me about life but also death and how I might tread the rough road of grief.

At the same time, my friends habitually ask me to read personal things I have written. I shared my journal with a few friends who said I should write a book on grieving. They said I convey what they cannot express in both joyful and challenging life situations. After thinking about turning my journal into a book, I realized it could serve others experiencing loss. Most don't know how to traverse the grieving process. Consequently, they choose to hold back tears and shove the feelings deep into the recesses of their hearts. However, I learned something through the loss of my dog. Hiding feelings is never conducive to the fullest enjoyment of life or helpful with healthy relationships.

Meanwhile, the writing journey changed me as a person and as an author. I cried every time I wrote as though I was reading someone else's book and learning from them. As a living example, I will guide you through the grieving process. I have learned how to grieve right along with you.

Later, when rewriting, I learned my primary aim in getting through the pain of loss was not to arrive at a joyful life again. Though that is one objective. It means so much more. You need to go through grief and all its associated tough emotions, instead of stuffing them like I was apt to do. It balances emotional energy. Some emotions feel good and some do not. Negotiating all emotions equals a transformed life. You become more in touch with your feelings and more prone to share them with loved ones and recognize them in others. This awareness opens up communication and enhances relationships. Consequently, you become grateful, focusing on the good rather than what is uncomfortable. Keep these long-range goals in mind as you read and digest *Floppy Ears*.

I learned a great deal about grieving as I wrote. The experience prepared me for an even greater loss—losing my husband-to-be, Danny. Grieving over my pet had been a hard-hitting and. valuable lesson, preparing me to lose my fiancé to a stroke on the date of our wedding. Losing a pet is devastating, but suddenly losing a loved one is beyond comprehension.

Similarly, I felt all I had experienced in my life prepared me for this day as Danny and I composed our wedding vows. Danny came into my life after eighteen years as a single mom. I was ready for this new chapter in my life. When Danny became sick two weeks before the ceremony date, I postponed every plan. Danny quickly became sicker and entered the hospital with Covid pneumonia. I contracted Covid the day after his admittance. I would remain extremely ill for three full weeks while Danny remained in the hospital.

Despite our illnesses, Danny and I talked on the phone multiple times daily as we prepared for him to come home. The doctor said he could return home within two days. It was never to be. On the long-awaited day of our wedding, blood clots lodged in Danny's brain and he suffered a stroke. He never regained consciousness. He died four days later. I never saw him again.

I began preparing for the memorial as soon as I recovered from Covid. All the while, I canceled plans for the wedding ceremony. The wedding was never to be. It felt weird to have only completed and memorized my vows to love, challenge, and respect Danny, only to be writing his eulogy a week later. It felt like yesterday that I joyfully wrote about how much Danny meant to me. As I wrote my tribute to Danny, I realized wedding vows and eulogies are alike to some extent. One contemplates what is special about that person you plan to spend the rest of your life with. Then, at their demise, you realize all that you loved about that person. Your tribute tells the world how much you cherished them. You will learn in this book how to write a tribute to those you love. It will change how you look at everyone you care about.

This book originated from the loss of my pet. However, after losing my husband-to-be, I realized what he had taught me in loving him, too. I bring Danny into this book so you realize the grief process is not only for the love and loss of a pet. It works just as well after losing a loved one. Much of the book will, however, be my journey after losing Paddy, my beloved Jack Russell, and how you can overcome the grief of your loss, too. You can use this process no matter what you have lost.

I have lost much in my life. However, I found that pain and grief transform you. It does not restore life before loss. Your life will never be the same. There will be differences.

It's a process. Negative emotions direct you in a way ignoring them never will and you become a better version of yourself.

It is deceptive to believe life will be simple and conflict-free. One must prepare for eventualities. *Floppy Ears* prepares you for the probabilities of life. Read my book, slowly taking in its nuances and direction. Let your feelings flow and don't hold back awareness of any emotions. Contemplate those reactions. Perhaps there are unsettled issues. You can deal with those too. Finally, mull over what I have written before moving on to the next chapter. Go back when you need to re-examine what I've said. And use a journal as I have. Have tissues ready. Be prepared to be transformed.

There are no words to express the heavy weight resulting from the pain of loss. One can hardly breathe. The weight of the world seems on your shoulders. This feeling will not last forever. May my journey through loss and pain guide you into a more enriching life for yourself and those around you. No matter where your story begins, you can write a new ending. Every ending is a new beginning. So goes the circle of transformation.

All *italicized* words are excerpts from my journal or quotes by others or myself.

~~~

*Boo–Ruthie Housman's beloved*

*"A loss not grieved is a life half lived."~Diana Lee~*

# CHAPTER 1
## Expert on grieving?

Most know nothing of grief. Do you? Sure, you may have grieved, but did you come out as a transformed person, knowing yourself better? Do you understand your feelings, relationships, gratefulness, and love more than before? Or did you muddle through brokenness just hoping to survive another day? Few embrace brokenness. Fewer even acknowledge it. Acknowledgment requires editing your thoughts, behaviors, and choices. Adding layers of understanding of your world necessitates work. However, who wants that much work when you are drowning in pain? It is hard to face ourselves. It is harder to change. The grieving process will change you. We all have known loss and pain, but not everyone knows how to overcome grief. **One aim of this book is to teach you to recognize when you have lost something and how to travel the emotional path toward acceptance, recovery, peace, and joy.**

Grief is a natural response to any loss in our lives. The pain of grief can touch us physically, emotionally, mentally, and spiritually. Although it is exhausting and unpredictable, every aspect and corner of it is natural. Grief causes one to realize life has not been what we hoped or expected. Even as I write this book, our entire planet is going through losses because of the harsh flu, Covid, threatening our way of life and the lives of loved ones. The Covid pandemic was unexpected and most do not wish to accept it and its ramifications. However, not everyone realizes Covid has brought many losses to our lives worthy of grieving. We all lost normalcy and many so much more. We need to grieve those losses no matter how exhausting. A revitalized body, a stabilized emotional state, mental clarity, an uplifted spirit, and soul renewal result from our hard work. Grief is a healthy process of coming to terms with loss and adapting and accepting reality. It is also about finding comfort. It's about putting your life back together again.

Whatever the loss, losing a loved one is the most devastating. The closer your bond to your loved one that has perished, the deeper the agony. Grief is the condition of loss. It is living without your loved one despite continuing emotional, psychological, or spiritual bonds. Therein lies the discomfort and resulting deep emotions. It is these uncomfortable feelings that define grief. No matter the loss, no one determines the magnitude of your loss but you. Only you know how much you hurt. It is you who tread the road, and the work involved in recovery.

We impede healing in an attempt to side-step suffering. Getting rid of pain is not heroic, but sadly a way around our true selves. The experience of feelings enriches our soul, who we are, and what we might become. Look carefully at what suffering reveals. We may need little else except to allow the soul room to breathe and grow through the suffering. Doing nothing but observing and allowing pain into the soul is one way to gain light and understanding of who we are. You will learn to do this in the part of my book, "becoming an emotional expert." Since I have lost so much, I should be an expert in grieving. I knew nothing going into this journey, but with my newfound knowledge, I have gained an experienced life of grieving and transformation. I shall never be the same.

In addition, this book is not only for pet owners. It's for anyone experiencing loss and doesn't know how to proceed. I arrived at many of my discoveries because of the loss of Paddy, my beloved Jack Russell. Similarly, I learned even more through the loss of my fiancé, Danny. We all have endured loss, not just of a pet or a loved one. Losses comprise a myriad of things; jobs, a way of life, families of divorce, a childhood, our dreams, or many other defeats. Even giving up a life of drugs and alcohol is a loss requiring a grieving process. Recovering alcoholics have lost their friends, identity, and lifestyle and it's painful, just like any other loss. Most associate grief with death, however, death is only one type of loss. One should grieve any adversity.

Although this book originated from the loss of my pet, I realized through the grief journey there were many losses in my life I never mourned. Equally, I see it in others' lives as well. You are in the right place if you experienced loss but didn't know it. Naturally, you're also where you should be if you don't understand how to grieve. Stick with me and you will learn how to grieve one step at a time.

Most everyone here on our planet can identify with pain. However, how many of us can pinpoint our defeat and deal with the excruciating hurt and disillusionment of grief? Losses can take a toll on our lives, driving sorrow so deep we can't reach it, let alone deal with it. We either stuff our pain and find something else to focus on or indulge in, or identify the feelings and respond in a healthy way. Painful situations transform us, turning pain into healthy individuals. If you have already encountered loss, either you dealt with it or you stuffed your emotions as I used to do. It is a life half-lived when we don't take time to grieve and pass through the pain.

It is through our brokenness that we come to a deeper understanding of ourselves. First, we must acknowledge the loss, name it, and understand what is happening with the barrage of emotions. We have to give ourselves permission to cry and go through the recovery stages. Telling yourself not to feel a certain way when you are suffering is not giving yourself the approval to negotiate all the conflicting emotions swirling around you. It is best to recognize something as a loss instead of letting it get buried within the grief. Overcoming loss comprises recognizing and acknowledging the pain and communicating with all your emotions. This is how one arrives at a more thorough understanding of oneself.

There is a process in which we learn about ourselves through our emotions. It is natural for you to want to hide from the pain. It is not a natural process to navigate the pain resulting from loss. Sometimes you don't know what to do with uncomfortable emotions. Although most don't want to experience what is called "negative emotions," all emotions transform us into someone better. All emotions our soul produces are part of who we are and how we process life. While the soul has a reason for the pain, it's not to seek immediate happiness. It doesn't benefit us from skipping the negative emotions of life. We ignore half of our emotional existence, thus half of who we are. The purpose of brokenness is not to break or destroy our spirits, but to refine us, bringing us into wholeness, maturity, and usefulness.

Likewise, every time we go through pain, we learn something new about ourselves, adding depths of meaning to our lives. It is much like a seven-layer chocolate cake. Richness adds up with each layer of the cake with its creamy frosting, holding each layer in place. Would you rather have a plain one-layer cake or a seven-layer chocolate cake with its height and depth? In my house, we choose the seven-layer cake every time.

Nonetheless, it helps to know the way to ride that roller coaster of grief. Professionals established the stages of grief. The experts have counseled a good many people through their pain. They know the way. Most of my book's chapters are stages guiding you on your journey. However, know the outline is only a guide. Each person's journey is unique, but it's useful to be aware of the stages. If you have endured loss, you will need guidance in executing the grief process. I have gone through them and outlined them in the coming chapters. Going through the emotions surrounding grief transforms us. Do you want to work through past losses and present ones? Are you willing to let those uncomfortable emotions change your life? If yes, read on.

Even if you have not lost a pet or a loved one, you can learn about grief. You will either encounter a loss before your life is over or you know someone who is going through some pain. My book is your chance to learn from all losses, learning about yourself and others. Mainly, you do not need to be an expert on grieving. Only be willing to recognize your emotions and advance through the pain and discomforts. Grief is the way life teaches you about yourself. Grieving transforms you into someone new, a better version of yourself. Challenging situations cause self-reflection and change. Because of grief, you know what you can handle. It is through the grief stages you realize how much more you think of love and what it means in your life. You will understand more about yourself and those around you.

Further, you will discover it is healthier to lament than not. Grieving loss is important to our health and relationships. Not grieving prevents your maximum capacity for happiness and peace, besides affecting your relations. Those who don't realize how to negotiate the grieving process and negotiate loss may forever experience difficulties recognizing emotions and dealing with relationships. If you do not move through the feelings involved in a loss, you may react over sensitively to small occurrences. You may end up angry or crying at the slightest provocation. Then you will wonder why you overreacted. You will not realize there are unresolved issues and emotions in your soul.

My book opens your eyes to the losses you have endured in the past. You may notice previous losses as you read *Floppy Ears*. There may be a pang of pain as emotions rise to the surface. Inspect your life for all the losses you never grieved. Go back through past losses and respond to their emotions. It is healthy to grieve old losses. Only you know if you have fully grieved the loss. As they appear in your memory or your heart, you will either feel intense pain, a dull ache, or even happiness if you have grieved and looked to the good you experienced in that relationship or other thing you lost. *Floppy Ears* teaches you gratitude if you have never been there after a loss. Grief is the path to a transformed you, whether it is the most recent loss or past loss.

One cannot help but learn about one's character as one takes on this quest. You will know who you were with your loved one and who you are becoming without your love. Equally important is taking the valuable aspects you learned from them and using them to make your world more enriching. If you look deep enough, you may notice what your pet taught you concerning relationships. Anyone can coach us on how to navigate relationships. There are oodles of books on the subject. Our dogs know how to love the day they are born. They love, for love's sake, are there in good times and bad, tail a-wagging when you reach home. Dogs and certain other pets are love's outstanding examples of love. You discover that love has risks. You could get hurt if you love. On the other hand, if you don't experience love, you miss a significant part of life. If you have never enjoyed a pet in your world, you have missed a vast part of growth, even when you lose them. You won't be the same after a loss.

There are more ways to grieve than professional opinions. Although, most experts agree that accomplishing relief and recovery from grief is through a process leading to acceptance, followed by eventual peace and joy. You will know what peace and joy mean to you. You will recognize them when they occur, just as you realize the other emotions involved in healing. All emotions work towards recovery, whether they are uncomfortable or enjoyable. All work towards emotional health.

Grief is a healthy process of coming to terms with loss, finding comfort, and adapting and accepting your reality. One of the most authoritative books on the subject noted by professional grief counselors is *"On Grief and Grieving."* Elisabeth Kubler-Ross, M.D., and David Kessler first established the five stages of grief. The counselors used the steps with terminally ill patients and later employed them in overcoming grief. There are more ways to overcome grief than the five stages. It is, however, the most widely known avenue of recovery. The stepping stones of recovery are the stages of grief. Or, as Ms. Kubler-Ross and Kessler state, it is *"finding the meaning of grief through the five stages of loss."* You can derive gain from what you lost and find the meaning in it all.

When you have suffered loss, I encourage you to admit it and move through the grief stages set up by the professionals. However, grief follows more of a process than progressing through steps. Dr. Kubler-Ross said near the end of her life that, "the stages were never meant to help tuck messy emotions into neat packages." It will become a rebuilding process where you can find a new meaning for your life as a whole person.

Grief is a process that teaches many lessons. Pain is the vehicle to ride that crazy, winding route to relief, growth, and comfort. *"People, once they know their emotions, can navigate the road themselves. They can drive their own car." (Thomas Moore, Care of the Soul)* Pain opens your eyes to the good in your world if you let it. You come to understand how to appreciate what you have, despite loss and pain. Gratitude brings great comfort. Being grateful will not eliminate the pain, but it will help you rise above to see other perspectives and options. This transition changes how you look at your situation. On the other side of mourning, there is growth in discovering joy. Your world becomes more abundant in meaning because you fathom how to grieve losses and understand your emotions. This awareness makes you more joyful and gracious in appreciation for what you enjoy in your heart. Then relief transcends all pain to let you know pain is not what you will forever know. There will be other emotions, some acceptable and others uncomfortable. But there are messages within those uncomfortable feelings. There is tremendous education gained through this transition. You transform into an extraordinary human being, knowing more of yourself than ever before. Know that your lessons will differ from mine. Each grief journey is not the end of the story. Your journey is the start of a fresh story, your story.

You don't need to be an expert to grieve, but knowing the way helps. I intend to take you on that journey toward relief. I am your escort with my progress through despair, and you will discover the framework to travel that road for yourself. Though the stages guide you, the journey is uniquely yours. Every emotion is commonplace when mourning. Likewise, there is no perfect approach to executing the steps. How you traverse the process, whether backward, forward, or upside down, is okay. My aim is for you to recognize your feelings and where you are on the emotional continuum as you navigate that path. It is like using your GPS to get to your destination. If you turn a different way, that voice utters, "Recalculating," but you still arrive at your destination. Grief can be on your terms.

It is through the experience of the loss of my pet and later my fiancé that I desire to guide you on your painful quest. I intend on you becoming a changed and better person through loss and pain. I will be there for you like no one else will. Not everyone you love will be there for you. We will go through this challenge together.

Despite my loss, I discovered joy throughout the grief journey as I recalled the many memories and lessons my dog showed me during our lives together. I also recovered memories and things my fiancé, Danny, taught me during our time together. As you review time with your pet or loved one, and if you allow it, you learn life lessons concerning relationships and death. I didn't realize what I had learned until Paddy, my dog, passed. Once he died, I found the treasures he left behind to discover, just as I used to leave him doggy treats to uncover while working. Suffering grief slows down our fast-paced world, giving us time to feel and heal.

Because I took the time to reflect, I found meaning in my soul. I realized there was more I could achieve. I don't do things as I did with Danny or Paddy. Each day is different. I have new goals, and yes, sadness remains at the prospect of going on without them. Conversely, there is joy in being someone new because of the sorrow I suffered. I will show you what Paddy taught me on my new journey. Likewise, you will find your path and discover a different person on the other side of sorrow. The new you will appreciate your world. You will know yourself better. Your relationships become enriched and life possesses value.

Because of letting emotions flow, you recognize what and who remains in your life. You choose who is worthy of your time and friendship. You can't miss the ones left to love. As you appreciate who enhances your world instead of taking away from it, you well up in gratitude and love. Your understanding and skills enable you to negotiate through emotions, love, and relationships. I show you how to express this love that changes your perspective on relationships. As a result, your relationships will flourish behind this new skill.

Besides all you learn about emotions, you will learn in *Floppy Ears* that it is okay to grieve a pet's death. You may feel silly for feeling so sad, but the loss is real. Death is not punishment or karma, but a reality of life, however painful. They were a soul tie, your companion, your family, and if you paid attention, your teacher. This was a live being enjoying daily life and its surprises with you. Consequently, you have lost a significant part of your heart and lifestyle. Your pet has forever transformed you and you have every right to mourn their loss. In fact, I discovered on the website; The Recovery Villiage.com/mental-health/grief/ that the effects of grief on the brain activate the same circuits in the brain as physical pain. Loss hurts!

It's equally important to remember not everyone will understand the love of a pet. Question who you trust to share your loss. Identify who will not understand or lend comfort. Regardless of some reactions to your pain, there is no shame in mourning a pet or whatever you deem a casualty. No one else can tell you what to grieve. It is your soul to tend to no one else's. Don't let others dictate your journey.

Furthermore, I have even grieved the loss of other people's pets. I was their auntie, you know, that person considered family because you come over so often. You fall in love with them and it becomes a loss when they pass from this life. It's natural to mourn any loss you consider a casualty. Don't skip this very important step even when you hear, "It's only a pet. You can get another." There is no shame in mourning the loss of a pet.

If you have a dog, you will understand my references better than if you own a cat or other pet. Your pet can be a horse, a dog, a cat, a turtle, or any pet you own. Cats don't love as dogs do, nor do turtles. Just bear with me and my dog associations, and you can still receive benefits from this book. Just know what you learn from your pet may differ from what your dog teaches you. Regardless of the pet you possess, pay attention, and you will recognize what your pet taught you about life, relationships, and death. We can

## Chapter 1

learn from all those around us, and our pets are no exception. They do not live as long as we humans because they already know what we take a lifetime to learn. *Floppy Ears* points to the view of the love and loss of a dog. You can learn from what a pet teaches you, especially following their passing. Sometimes, it is the love of a pet that teaches us about human love. As you realize lessons from a simple pet, you see lessons everywhere.

My brother, Kevin, and his wife Venus have a goat named Sunny and a miniature pony they dress up for every occasion. The goat lives indoors. Yup, he does.

*Sunny*

*Mischa–Tena Clark's kitty*

Bereavement is a choiceless event. You are going through something you don't understand or even like. It was not your choice to be in the grieving position. However, you can explore it or suppress the pain. You have that choice. Admitting grief is one step towards relief. Also, part of admittance is knowing you are in control of nothing but your reactions. It can seem like holding a soaking wet cat in a paper bag. Let the emotions flow. Let the cat out of the bag. Release the tight hold on your agony and see beyond the pain. All emotions hold some value. **Pain and joy both hold equal value in the scheme of recovery.** (Repeat that last sentence out loud to yourself) When you can hold your head above the misery, you will see beyond the sorrow.

The root word of bereavement is "reave," which means "torn apart." It is like putting a puzzle together. When you dump out the pieces on the table, you must sift through and

# Chapter 1

place them, making a recognizable picture. Like the pieces of a puzzle, you are taking your spiritual and emotional pieces and putting them back together for wholeness in your soul.

I include many ideas in *Floppy Ears* that may change your perspective on death and sorrow, too. It is these experiences and emotions that cause growth. You will know how to recognize and experience emotions. The result is freedom, the freedom to know yourself and be yourself. Part of being yourself is knowing who and what to grieve, who and what is important to love, and what to let go. As you do the work, pain will lose its tight grip on your heart. Some say, "Time heals all wounds." However, in my eyes, it is you who heal yourself from the grief of your loss. Take all the time you need. This book is for those who will learn from emotional pain, who have lost something special in their life, but desire joy to arise from the ashes of sorrow.

I don't pretend to be an expert on bereavement. I wrote in a journal to control my despair at having lost one of the best things in my world, my pupster. Later, it became the loss of my love. My world has been richer because of the painful rollercoaster. Quite a metamorphosis took place as I routinely entered into my notebook. Journaling helped ease the pain. It gave me a backward glance at life and how much I had transformed. Paddy instructed me regarding living a full life and appreciating my relationships and time. Most importantly, I grasped how to grieve. In learning to lament, I detected many losses in my life that I did not deem important enough to grieve. I observed how I stuffed the emotions, displayed a stiff upper lip, and went on with living as though I was okay. I wasn't. Not living through the emotional turmoil had hampered my joy in living and the richness of relationships. Grief not dealt with is a life half lived. Furthermore, I have learned through my grief experience how to live fully after loss. Time allowed me to see clearly. My knowledge resulted from journaling and contemplation. The loss was not the end of my story. It is my new beginning.

This book is my wandering through the grief journey. I did not intend it to be professional advice. Though I am a more experienced griever than a professional grief counselor, I specialized in counseling classes in college and studied some theories used for grief counseling. Later, I gave the subject some attention through books written by other experts. However, I never gave grieving much thought until I began writing concerning my loss and accompanying feelings. Put on paper, the process became clear. As I discovered the many ways we grieve, I saw the value in the process. My book outlines the five stages by professionals and a couple of my own. Also, how I negotiated the stages, and how you can too. This book is not a replacement for treatment after a pet or loved one's death if you need it. This book expresses my grief. I am not the grieving expert, only the experienced griever. It is through my experience with grief that what I valued crept back into my soul. In fact, I now recognize grief in others and can extend compassion and comfort because of what I have learned and experienced. It is like my heart broke open and compassion spilled out. That occurrence may not have happened had I not felt that excruciating pain and subsequent relief and healing.

# Chapter 1

Further, I am confident you will discover what you value and how to achieve meaning through the grieving process, just as I did. Finding meaning in your existence is how peace and joy evolve through emotions, love, and relationships. You decide how to live the remaining portion of your life and with whom. Your life is livelier and full of meaningful interactions. Likewise, your soul differs from before your loss. My world has been richer, having Paddy and later Danny in my life. Losing my best friends has been difficult. What I learned through that reality is invaluable. I am more appreciative of all I have to share and enjoy. Likewise, I believe you will conclude that over time, too. It doesn't feel like it yet but get started and you will grow and mature.

Whether you have lost a loved one or a pet, or you lost a lifestyle because of the Covid virus, you grieve but might not recognize it. Knowledge from my book offers you direction on your path. This book guides you through the grieving process so you can discover your path after loss. This is a fresh path with new experiences you did not expect. It will be a new you walking that road through the tough emotions—the ones you don't want to go through, transform you, not destroy you. An analogy of growth resulting from pain is like a power lifter. If the weight lifter did not increase the weight lifted, he would never get stronger muscles. The same is true of trials. The tough struggles we endure strengthen us, too. We transform from weaklings who believe we can't take the weight of the pain to healthy people able to live through our suffering. This growth prepares us for future defeats. Our adversities refine us, causing us to be compassionate about others' suffering. The purpose of trials is to better ourselves, not destroy us. Trials grow us in understanding the hurts of others and how we can assist. However, it is work you must be willing to complete.

Then you can apply what you gained through grief and identify how to deliver consolation to others. Your compassion will flourish and spread to others around you. Comfort and empathy are lessons well received and go far in enhancing any relationship. Dealing with feelings strengthens relationships, as is also expressing those feelings. Declaring your emotions and learning from emotional pain leads to the healing process. Those who lost something special in their life can discover joy from the ashes of sorrow. During grief, you may feel you will barely get through another sunset. Take one step and see what's next.

Lastly, I suggest you write in a journal and contemplate what you discover regarding yourself and your journey. Many thoughts swirl around your head, but when pen goes to paper, the subconscious takes over and finishes those theories. You see more on paper than you organize inside your brain. The specialists call this self-care. Care of oneself is imperative in any emotional life situation. I urge you to receive the many methods of self-care within *Floppy Ears.* I have included many ideas for self-care in the Index. This can mean anything from letting loose with tears to talking about your pain to someone you trust not to judge you. Hire a therapist if you think you require it, but read this book first. Your fullest, most meaningful life may depend on it. You may require help along the road, but at least you will realize your course.

**My purpose for writing is to encourage you to see that if you have suffered the loss of a person, pet, or anything you consider a disaster, it's best to recognize the upset, then move through the grief, gaining from the experience.** The overall benefit of my book is finding a way through grief. However, the transformation results in a more grateful and compassionate you. Your life will become full of meaning and rich relationships. My book is about becoming a better person because of the trials and pain.

Before we get into the meat of the book and the process of healing, I want to introduce you to the day I lost Paddy. You will know my pain and understand that I may experience the same depth of pain you are experiencing. You will understand the love of my pet, just as I understand the love of yours.

*"God works on us as we journey, grow, and learn to live through these life events for which we are never ready." ~Diana Lee~*

~~~

# The Day Paddy Died

*"When we adopt a dog or any pet, we know it is going to end with us having to say goodbye, but we still do it."* ~W. Bruce Cameron~

With a heavy and hurting heart, I write to inform you about my dog Paddy's death. I came home from work, and just like any day. Paddy was underfoot looking for morsels in the dirt I swept up and at the kitchen counter waiting for tidbits of food to drop upon his head. I took him for a short walk up the driveway, and he ran down the hill, his little ears a-flopping, not appreciating the stroll, just wanting to get inside the door to the warmth of our home. His old bones no longer enjoyed romping through the snow in the chill of winter.

After finishing my chores and dinner, I sighed, ready to relax. Paddy kept going to the door, standing patiently, waiting for me to let him out. He was a little more wobbly than usual on his feet; it seemed. After letting him out for the umpteenth time, he came in and puked up a few times. I busied myself cleaning up his messes letting him out one more time. When I looked out after him, I noticed there was diarrhea on the ground as he stumbled towards the door. I gingerly picked him up, carried him in, and put him on the kitchen counter to clean him up. He deserved dignity. I scrutinized him to find the source of his inability to walk. One of his back legs was dangling uselessly. I set him on the floor, but he kept collapsing helplessly. I picked him up again and hid him in his bed under his blanket. He didn't seem to want to stay in his bed but kept attempting to get up, sliding around feebly. I sobbed at my powerlessness to help him. He was crying, and I was crying. I was hoping it was something temporary. That was wishful thinking in full denial that something serious was wrong.

Through his crying, I managed to call my vet only to receive the message to phone an emergency animal hospital down the hill. The caring hospital spoke compassionately, giving me direction. I loaded Paddy snugly in his blanket. It was the only way to lift him as he bit at my flesh in his misery. I would take the bites, knowing that was all he could communicate. I cooed softly to him as he cried over the miles to the hospital. It seemed like an eternity as I hastened my drive behind every slow driver. Finally, I arrived and bundled him up, and took him in. Blood covered Paddy's face and toes from scutching across the floor, hitting all the furniture's legs. He immediately stopped crying, letting me hold him tenderly. He somehow knew I would take care of him, just as I had always done. After all these years together, he trusted and believed in me.

They took him immediately after they took my information before I could even plop wearily down in the crowded hospital. I caressed another dog while I waited for the vet. Perhaps I was giving him what I wanted to share with my pupster. Or I just wanted to love that dog who was about to go over that rainbow bridge himself. It doesn't matter. He soaked up my love contentedly.

I texted a friend who loved "Paddy Bear" and had cared for him a million times while I traveled to another state. It was my fortune and God's miracle that my friend was only a short distance *away. The attendant called me into the vet's office. No Paddy. The small room appeared to be for consultations. The vet explained what I still don't understand. Something had burst in the spine, causing a clot and a heart murmur, resulting in paralysis. The vet delicately spoke while he explained what they could do for Paddy. It didn't sound hopeful, and when I expressed that to him, he agreed. He conveyed he had two dogs himself and would not let his dogs go through the trauma if they had so many good years already. I agreed with his assessment, then decided Paddy had had enough fun and love to put him through any more pain and things he did not understand. I wanted his suffering to end, and that meant ending his life.*

*Momentarily, my good friend's round face showed through the window of the room where I sat. He observed me for a moment, evaluating, taking in my countenance, and my emotions, thinking about how best to proceed. For anyone who knows how to love, he surrounded me in his arms and didn't say a word. His comfort was almost more than I could bear. There were so many emotions swirling around in me at that moment. It was the sweetest gesture of love. It was then that I verbalized what I had decided. He didn't question my decision, but knew I had made the right one for Paddy, whom he loved dearly. There are no contests in love. No one cares more or less than another. We all love how we know best to love.*

*Choosing to end Paddy's life has been the most natural and most challenging decision in my life. Who are we to decide when a person or a pet should be with God? We are not God. However, our overwhelming love speaks to us, telling us our pets don't understand the pain and suffering they are experiencing. Everything they experience is through us, their beloved owners. Every need they have revolves around us fulfilling those needs and desires. They look to us for what's best for them. Intuitively, our pets only know how to give their loyal love but are resigned to receiving what we offer, good, bad, or indifferent. It is in our compassion and love that we treat them humanely.*

*Death is a very sacred time to share with someone you love so much during their last breaths. I will never forget our final moments together. We gazed deep into each other's eyes, communicating more than I could ever express. I am sure there will be understanding, love, and comfort in heaven, all without words. He knew I held his life in my hands and heart. He knew I would do the best for him, regardless of how selfish I could be in putting him through more torment and a life he no longer wanted to live. Paddy only lived for me. I reassured him over and over how much I loved him, kissing his ears and face as I had every day of his life. I massaged him, touching him for the last time, his paws limp in my hand in complete surrender. I reassured him it would soon be over as soon as I could let go and say goodbye.*

*An hour after Paddy died, I decided it was time to walk out that door into the night and begin my grieving. It would be a long drive home to the mountains only forty minutes away. It would be the longest drive of my life, knowing that Paddy would not rise to greet me when I returned. The house would smell of him, but there would be no clicking of his toenails upon the hardwood floor coming to find me in the darkness.*

*For anyone who knew and loved Paddy, they realized he took over our home, any house really, with his love and presence. His presence was enormous, with his big dog attitude in his small puppy body. My house bears a transformation as much as I will be forever changed by knowing and loving him. I uncannily knew my life would take shape differently this year.* Zac, my son, left only Sunday and ultimately vacated his room on Monday. Paddy died two days later. I still have not told him of Paddy's death. I want to talk to him in person. The two of them grew up together. They were brothers. Even though there was sibling rivalry, Zac will know loss too. He, however, will never know how alone I am now.

When I arrived home, I left the lights off, not wanting to see everything Paddy left behind, the remnants of his life, his bed, his blanket, his dishes. My eyes could not bear to take in the things that would distract me from those eyes that considered me so loving and trusting in his last moments. I wanted to watch the moon descend behind the mountain beyond and not let this day go. I didn't want it to be over the day Paddy went to meet his real master. I did not want to greet another day as though my life had not changed in all I had experienced in that short time. The smell of Paddy wrapped around me as I slept on the couch that night. I could not sleep in my bed, my feet not touching his body stretched across the mattress, taking up all the room. He had this way of saying, "I'm here, so don't forget it!" He always wanted to be the boss. In his way, he was. My life revolved around him in every way, in every consideration. I will let him forever be the boss if that is what it takes to get him back.

It was no mistake that my friend was blessfully close upon this crisis with Paddy. God knows what He is doing, and His timing is right. I don't understand it but must accept it. After all, how can death ever be just at the right time, and yet it is? If you think about it, we are never ready for anything we encounter in life; marriage, children, school, work, retirement, and death. God works on us as we journey, grow, and learn to live through these life events. He equips the "called" for life. He does not call the equipped. Who *knows better than our creator how to prepare each one of us? Only He knows what we will have to endure.*

*In my previous life, I would have let no one in to comfort me. I would have struggled in pain alone, overwhelmed with grief. God has stretched and grown me into a more compassionate person who will comfort others and allow comfort from others. His journey for me is ongoing. He prepares me for what is ahead. I must walk the road He places before me. I am thankful now He has put those who love me in my way. We don't know where that avenue will lead, but each day begins with one step, "through fields and over bridges, into that long walk into forever..."*

You must have felt my pain as you read about the day my dog Paddy died. Perhaps you have already lost your beloved pet, or a loved one of the humankind. You already know the pain, or you own a pet and know that someday they will meet their creator as Paddy did on that fateful day. Perhaps you initially picked up this book because of the cute picture of Paddy as a pupster on the cover and the equally captivating title. You thought the book to be about more puppy dog tales and entertaining stories about someone's pet. We have seen many of these when we view pet books. However, when you read the subtitle, *How to overcome grief from loss, and other life lessons I learned from my pet*, you paused. Perhaps you experienced a tug on your heart from past pain. Maybe you will realize some lessons you have learned from your pet. Mostly, you understand that there has been some loss in your life, and perhaps you never knew how to deal with it.

Points to consider:

- Grief is a natural response to loss, but overcoming grief usually needs to be learned.
- No one can determine your loss but you. Loss can be a pet, a loved one, or anything else.
- We impeded healing by ignoring our pain.
- We learn through emotions. All emotions are useful for transformation.
- The purpose of brokenness is not to break or destroy your spirit but to refine you.
- Love has risks, such as loss, but is a significant part of living and learning.
- Getting through grief is not just about arriving at acceptance, peace, and joy.
- Overcoming loss also aids in relationships and helping others through their loss.
- Overcoming loss will lead to a more healthy you!

You will learn in the coming chapters what a pet becomes to us and how they fill our lives with love and acceptance. You will learn to see the lessons not only our pets have for us, but what their loss, all losses have to teach us.

*"If there are no dogs in Heaven, then when I die, I want to go where they went." ~Will Rogers~*

~~~

*Buckshot Jeff & Teresa's pup*

*"Before you get a dog, you can't quite imagine what living with one might be like; afterward, you can't imagine living any other way." -Caroline Knapp~*

# Chapter 2
# Pet or Friend?

Pets become our friends even before we realize the connection, no matter how we come by them. Are they your pet or a friend? You decide. For me, it is those we share our lives with who become our friends. Our friends can and many times become our family, the family we choose.

When we deliver our new pet home, we think of them as just a pet. Somehow, we believe we own them. We don't know when they move in and take over our space; they will become more later, and we don't own them after all. It happens so gradually; we don't notice. We don't know they will feel like family to us. Many people even sign the dog's name on holiday cards given to others. I have. Leaving out the family's pet would be like leaving out a family member. The dictionary defines a pet as "a domestic or tamed animal kept for companionship or pleasure." They grow on us and become our friends and our family. Our pets teach us how to be good friends. They teach us to love unconditionally. They do that and so much more.

Here is an excerpt from my journal demonstrating unconditional love.

*Paddy gave me the kiss of life. He never was the kissing type, but he gave me the kiss of life in the end. He showed me unconditional love. That sounds like a cliché, but there are few places where we genuinely receive love and are never asked for anything in return than the love of pets. I am incredibly blessed to see the miracle of unconditional love, and it is a miracle. Our natures are selfish and always in want. To give love without expecting or even wanting love in return is human nature. We love to receive love. However, our pets love us merely to love. Paddy gave me that kiss of life without a touch.*

I believe unconditional love is the foremost lesson our pet teaches us. Friendship is the second. Merriam-Webster defines a friend as "Attached to another through affection or esteem, a favored companion." A favored companion would encompass a friendship, would it not? Comrade is another word for companion. Comrades associate through a joint mission or interest. We don't always know what purpose it will serve in our relationships until we travel that journey. We don't know what impact a pet in our lives will have either. When our pets become our friends, we go into the unknown, learning and growing together. We will both learn about life and death and the growing relationship in between.

Both definitions of pet and friend encompass a relational bond. One description speaks of animals kept but with companionship attached. The friend definition does not speak of a human-to-human relationship—only one connects to another through bonding. Who says that a bond cannot be with one's dog or pet? Who has not heard of a dog as a man's best friend? Both definitions speak either of companionship, pleasure, or mutual affection. I think all those characteristics permeate both friendships and pet attachments.

If we pay attention, pets teach us much about relationships. They teach us how to be good friends. They know how to choose good friends better than we do. My dog either growled or wagged his tail upon meeting someone new. Pets know how to be loyal. They are always there for us, no matter what. Pets are more trustworthy than most of our best friends. They are there rain or shine, good days, or bad days. If you don't test them too much with your steak lying around on a plate, they are trustworthy, as the day is long. They bring comfort when we are sad or upset. Being around for us to caress calms us down. Dogs know how to live in the moment, and play at a moment's notice. They help us know when it's time to take a break. Anytime is a good time for dogs to pause from their busy days to frolic and catch a few sticks. They also don't judge and help us learn to be grateful for who is in our lives without criticizing them. Most of all, our pets teach us unconditional love. They will love us no matter how we treat them, if we don't feed them or stay away too long. They love us regardless of our follies and imperfections. If we followed a dog's example of friendship, we would never lack good friends.

*"The world would be a nicer place if everyone had the ability to love as unconditionally as a dog." ~M.K. Clinton~*

There is the question of how much we own our pets. Look around you. Do their toys, beds, and bowls speak to the presence of a pet? They take over our homes. Then, over time, they take hold of our hearts and, thus, own us. Friends and pets come to us in many ways. How did you come by your pet? Did you save it, or did they rescue you? Did you decide to go to the pound and liberate a pet from annihilation? Perhaps your child brought one home from school. Did one show up at your door or come by a friend's or neighbor's hand with new puppies? Did it choose you, or did you choose it? We don't always choose our friends and don't always choose our pets, either. Some stay and some do not, but those who stay can and most often become our family.

It doesn't matter how your relationship came to be. It matters most how you forge that relationship. This kinship is a bond of mutual affection. How would you cultivate that bond? Will you expect your pet to learn to go potty outside,

## Chapter 2

stay off the furniture, and mind you but not learn from them at the same time? If you thought when you received your pet, they would only learn from you; you would be sadly mistaken. Pets have much to teach us about love, relationships, life, and death, no matter how we gained them.

This is how I came by my pet, Paddy, how he came by his name, and how he became more than a pet.

*I remember the day we received Paddy as clearly as this moment in time. We were celebrating my wasband's birthday. The adorable spotted puppy was his gift. Paddy was only eight weeks old and as small as a hamster. Everyone adored Paddy the moment they laid eyes on him. All the children had poor Paddy corralled as if he was a creature in a circus there to entertain them. I knew Paddy was tired of being so cute and entertaining, and soon, the parents were thankfully taking their children away to bed. All the partiers had retired to their rooms at the hotel nearby and were fast asleep, except for a few men who continued to make haste with a bottle of Irish whiskey. I got into bed, ready for the night to close its veil over my eyes to rest. It had been a long day of preparation for the party. I put Paddy, the new puppy, in my son Zac's bed, hoping they would become fast friends. Who wouldn't want their child to know the love and responsibility of a pet? Soon after closing my eyes, I made out muffled grunts and scratching at my bed. I tried to ignore the commotion, but the noise soon drowned the drinking men's drunken laughter. I waited to see what the clamor was all about when Paddy hurdled himself upon the mattress and pranced over to where I lay, plopping down beside me with a sigh of accomplishment. Paddy had selected me to be his companion until he departed from this world into his, but forever in my heart.*

St Paddy's day and how I named my dog.

*Today I was telling a friend how Paddy received his name. How à propos that it was St Patrick's Day when I relayed the story. Paddy came as a birthday gift, but not to me. Since the men were drinking the Irish Whiskey, we brought back from Ireland; his name became Paddy. The part of the Irish in me said, "Okay," that fits. He behaved feisty as the red-haired Irish, determined to get his way, always competitive and ALWAYS won, vigorous as any fighting Irish, love deep in his dark Irish eyes. His eyes bored intensely and looked deep into your soul. You could not look into his eyes and not be changed. If you looked into his eyes, you just communicated with a dog. Oops, what dog? He would never have admitted he was a dog, and I would never admit that dog was my best friend.*

I would never know how Paddy would become such a fast and reliable companion as I went through a divorce and total financial ruin. Left with two hundred dollars and no place to live, I had to make a home for my son, dog, and myself. I needed emotional support and courage to make it through the wreckage of my life. My dog became the most loyal and consistent part of my life during that time. Luckily, he chose me. If I had known I would need his loyal companionship, I would have wanted him instead of pawning him off on my son. As a single mom, I required that solidarity to shore up the devastation from the divorce. I never knew how much that dog would mean to me or how much he would teach me about life and relationships. I trained my dog to do many cute tricks, but he educated me so much more than I ever taught him.

As I look back upon our lives, I realize I thought he would always be with me through my trials and tribulations. In the end, I also realized that he taught me even more through his death. It was then I discovered the miracle of birth and death.

*Through the life Paddy gave me, I discovered death is a miracle as much as birth is a gift. They define a miracle as improbable, an extraordinary event, not in the typical scheme of life. However, birth and death are quite ordinary and happen every day. When we see a baby breathing its first breath outside the womb, wailing in the cold, unprotected place of its mother's warmth, we beam with delight. Why wouldn't we do the same as the spirit leaves the burden of the body as it takes its last breath into freedom and an unencumbered life? Is it not just such a gift? It is a miracle to see rest and peace in the face of those who pass on as it is to see new life in the eyes of a baby who coos and tries out its new fingers, feeling the presence of others? Should we not be in awe that the spirit is somewhere beyond our physical reach? Can we not find delight in the spirit's freedom to live beyond the burden of pleasing us and trying to communicate in our imperfect world? It would seem logical that we would mourn the birth of a child who will grow up and learn lessons the hard way, deal with pain and imperfect love and communication, and rejoice at death, with its peace, rest, and freedom, never to hurt again. I'm learning that even though both are miracles, we rejoice in one and dread the other. Though we see life and death as regular occurrences, we still measure them as a miracle. I consider a miracle the work of a divine agency that no human can control. Life and death must then be a divine intervention, a real blessing, an extraordinary event. Though I could try to rejoice in Paddy leaving his encumbered body for a life of freedom, I just can't. I can only celebrate those moments we shared as friends, and I still celebrate the day he was born.*

Discovering I am not the only one who considers their pet family.

*Today, on my run, I ran into a neighborhood couple who consistently take their walks in our local mountains. When I stopped to chat, they directly inquired about Paddy. Though I do not get emotional as I did earlier, their question blindsided me, as I believed all my neighbors would know by now about Paddy's demise. I explained what happened, and they responded empathetically. They have had pets. They know how it feels to lose a beloved family member, as they referred to our pets. Pets indeed become our family. We spend time with them in every capacity on a day-to-day basis. They know our schedules, our follies, our emotions, and our aptitude for playfulness. They know us as any family member would. Many, these days, take their dogs everywhere. I see them on the plane, in Home Depot, our home improvement supply stores, in outdoor restaurants, parks, and on boats. I took Paddy everywhere with me except on planes. He was a well-behaved, potty-trained dog, welcomed by all my friends. Upon arrival at our destination, he would sniff around, and when he had inspected our new residence, he would plop down in his bed and call it home for a spell. Paddy secured the spot as the current family member. Families are the friends you choose, right? Or is that friends are the family you choose? Either way, that works for me.*

*We were a pair. He was my friend, my best buddy, and my family. We did everything together. I have not walked down to the pond, up the hill behind my house, or over the rocks where we would lounge in the sun, watching the clouds overhead. If I had to hike without my companion, I could not endure it. I cannot brave a walk without Paddy. I never walked by myself. I didn't live solo. With Paddy by my side, I didn't have to face life alone.*

## Chapter 2

*When we were hiking in the National Forest bordering our home, you would think Paddy would want to run about and sniff and chase little critters. Nope. Whenever we stopped to rest and contemplate life and watch the clouds drift by, he would roost on my lap, or knees, wherever he had a good view of all there was to see, even if my perch was on the edge of the cliff. He completely trusted that if I choose to sit there, it would be safe. He would be safe.*

*One hot summer day, Paddy and I climbed up high on some rocks on a hilltop looking out over the valley and surrounding mountains. There was no path to follow. The view was worth the hike and scramble. Paddy and I made our way through the brush and over rocks. We sat down to rest and took in the view for a spell. When we rose to leave, I heard a rustling sound. I looked over to see the hugest Rattler I have ever seen coiled and blending into the rock's color where it lay. We sat there for a long time without ever seeing or disturbing it. We scurried to get as far away from its domain as possible when I suddenly heard that characteristic rustling sound again. Right where we had taken the route to the top of the rocks was another rattlesnake! I stumbled over myself, trying to find another way out of his path. Since it was only a pile of boulders on our course, I jumped up over another rock and got the heck out of there! My heart didn't stop pounding until I was safe in my home. I had picked up Paddy, and he was never the wiser. I think we ran all the way home as if the two rattlesnakes were hot on our trail. Now, if that wasn't good for the heart and blood flow, I don't know what is!*

We did everything and went everywhere together. When our pets die, they leave such a hole in our lives where they used to always be. Ultimately, it is those we spend our time with that become our friends and family. I spent most of my time with Paddy. He was my friend, companion, comrade, family member, and teacher. He taught me about life, relationships with humans, and death more than anyone I know. Pets fill a purpose in our lives, no matter how we gain them. Pets serve a purpose on life's journey even after they die. The life we lived together will forever imprint them into our souls.

## Points to consider:

- It is who we spend time with who becomes our friends and family.
- Our pets can teach us so much about life, relationships, and death.
- We learn from our pets the miracle of unconditional love.
- It doesn't matter how you came by your relationship, but how you forge that relationship.

The next chapter discusses the intricacies of death and what we believe about life after death. Experiencing death has the direct result of slowing us down long enough to contemplate the important things in life. Coming to know what we believe will bring us not only something to believe in, but the comfort we require.

*"Dogs are not our whole life, but they make our lives whole.*
*–Roger Caras~*

~~~

*"Pets are such agreeable friends. They ask no questions and tell no lies." ~Diana Lee~*

*Picture of Harley (Kathryne's dog) telling no lies*

*Asked if he did "it" and he just smiles*

*"When I look into the eyes of an animal, I don't see an animal. I see a living being. I see a friend. I feel a soul."*
~Anthony Douglas Williams~

# CHAPTER 3
# Life After Death

The important part of death is knowing what you believe happens to someone after their passing. Whatever your religious or spiritual beliefs, all have experienced loss and pain and must handle the emotions surrounding that loss. Part of those emotions may be uncertainty concerning life after death for yourself and your loved one. I speak of God and life after death in *Floppy Ears*. If my religious beliefs offend you, this book is not for you. Conversely, this book is for you if you believe in eternal connections, as I do. However, you can learn to navigate the stages of grief even if you believe this life is all we get on earth and when you die, any essence of you dies, too. Alternately, you may believe you return to earth in another body to relive and learn your lessons. Despite your spiritual or religious beliefs, only you can determine how one completes the end of life. You might never have considered how loss can co-exist with gain. I want you to be confident in your beliefs. I will urge you many times in this book to find what you believe about life after death to aid your healing. The time of death is not the moment to be contemplating and stressing over where one goes after death.

When you know what life after death means to you, you have a better understanding of death and how to negotiate its turmoil. When you solidify your beliefs, you also find what you value in life. It is in taking the time required to contemplate these issues that will eventually bring you comfort within the pain. When you accept the reality of loss and make adjustments to your world, you begin to see some things you never considered until now. Life has a way of teaching us lessons from experiences, whether we consider them good or bad. It's all perspective. Because of what you learn, you will be prepared for future losses which we can count on. There is comfort in knowing what you believe and value, but it takes contemplation and time. It is to your benefit to take that time before death enters your life. All the work you do towards understanding your beliefs will go a long way in recovering from grief.

*Floppy Ears* will cause your mind to see other perspectives and mingle them with your own beliefs to arrive at new ideas and bring you comfort. You do not have to change your beliefs. Rather, I cover my perspective so you understand what has worked for my understanding and comfort during loss. I maintain even when considering other perspectives on death, the stages of grief, developed by professionals, will work for anyone willing to get through the tough emotions and administer self-care. I believe anyone experiencing loss resulting in pain and the other myriad of emotions should execute the way through until they become someone they weren't before the loss. Eventually, the process of grieving should solidify your beliefs and what you value most in life.

Have you ever contemplated the death of yourself, a loved one, or a pet? You either determined what happens when someone dies or are not sure. Your uncertainties concerning death can cause fear to settle over you in a haze when you contemplate the inevitable. To feel at ease with death, you must decide where your beliefs lie concerning life after death to bear the most comfort. Because I am certain in my heart and mind about the end of life as we know it on earth, I am comforted by my belief that our body dies but our spirit lives on. There are other aspects of my Christian beliefs that also comfort me. Some are conscious, some are not. However, I believe you can carry any religious or spiritual beliefs and still learn to grieve any losses that occur for you. You can incorporate what you learn from *Floppy Ears* into your religious and spiritual practices. This chapter is not an exhaustive study concerning death or the afterlife. However, you will know how I handled grief and incorporate what you believe into your own experience. In conclusion, it is of utmost importance to know what you believe before death. This will bring the most comfort.

Here is an excerpt from my journal describing what it feels like to lose someone but be uncertain about what happens when they die. It is painful to observe a person close to you live through the uncertainties of death.

*It has been a month since my last entry in my journal. I put my grieving aside somewhat for a friend who lost her husband. I can't tell her, "I understand how you feel" because losing a spouse is not like losing a pet. However, I understand some feelings relating to being alone. Or coming home to an empty house. Nothing is the same because they are not with you on adventures. I know the emptiness and the pain of loss. I understand the longevity of a relationship you cultivated in understanding the other and making accommodations based on those understandings. I can relate to being uncomfortable around jovial people when you just want to cry. I fathom crying for no apparent reason, just out of the blue of the sky and the green of the grass. My friend doesn't know if she will see her love after her life here on earth is complete. She had so many questions.*

*We live expectantly for relief and answers to our painful questions. Will we see them in their youth and vigor? Will they be waiting to run across the bridge between life and death when they glimpse us in our youthful bodies waiting for that long-awaited hug? We question whether we will see our loved ones after we die. Our dog, our person, was good. Don't they deserve a healthy life after death? Will they have healthy bodies? Before a spouse dies, there are questions to ponder. Don't wonder and hope they are in a better place. My friend's pain, not knowing if she would see her spouse after her death, was almost more torment than I could endure. In the end, the uncertainty was her cross to bear, even though I cried along with her. I have peace in believing I will see my beloved Paddy and Danny after my life is over. That peace is a treasure to hold, whether or not it is true. We all need to believe in something.*

My friend had so many questions that I could not answer for her. Eventually, we have to ask and answer our own questions. No one can answer life's questions for you. The time for learning and philosophical judgments is before tragedy strikes. The shock is too great for your emotional and psychological system if you wait to contemplate life's mysteries during a tragedy. How you react to anything you encounter in life depends on developed thoughts and attitudes beforehand. Before someone passes from this world, know what you believe. The process of grief will be easier to execute if you eliminate this one big stumbling block.

Knowing what you believe about life after death is only one example of circumstances to contemplate concerning life. Although I cover "the meaning of life" in Chapter eleven, it needs to be introduced here since inspecting death and its repercussions is part of finding meaning in one's life. I believe life is random and pointless without life after death. That concept means God created us without a purpose. It is our purpose that gives meaning to living. My comfort is believing that I'm going to another world. Those I love will be there to greet me. It has taken me years of contemplation and meditation to arrive at my conclusions. My beliefs greatly comfort me and add meaning to my life.

It's difficult to get in touch with yourself in our hustle, bustle world. Who has time to ponder life's mysteries? Our physical, material world stares us in the face every day. Materialistic things give us something to do or act upon. We have work, children to care for, homes to attend to, and relationships to cultivate, not to mention having a bit of fun. Thinking beyond ourselves and superficiality is hard. However, depth of thought is worth the time and solitude it takes to cultivate. We can become transcendent in a superficial world. Depth is infinite and gives life and death meaning. When we have meaning, we don't live by chance, but by design. Meanwhile, we chose how to react and behave because we decided who we want to be or become, and what we believe. Living intentionally brings pleasure and happiness because there aren't so many uncertainties. We have clarity of thought and faith in our beliefs. Rather, we are no longer passive bystanders in life but participants. Understanding life's secrets gives us power. We no longer need to fear life or death. We know how to catch a curveball and what to do with it. Our reactions will be mostly certain. I know how to respond in most situations because of my age and experience. Furthermore, forethought has supplied me with guidelines. My religion has also gifted me guidelines, but my spirituality picks up where conscious thought and religious doctrine leave off.

Since religion and spirituality relate to the meaning of life, I must clarify what I mean by those two subjects so you will understand the differences and similarities, but also how I define the two practices. Your definitions may be as unique as you are, but here I offer my interpretation. Both practices intend to bring purpose, meaning, and peace to one's life. We encounter the meaning of one's life in everyday challenges, but I believe we need something to base our values, decisions, and actions upon during those challenges. Both positions are an avenue to the meaning of life and what we value and, thus, how we respond to circumstances.

Religion and spirituality are neither the same nor completely separate. On one hand, religious beliefs are based on a set of specific practices that revolve around a god or person and often a set of written words encompassing those beliefs and practices. Religion is shared within a group of individuals or practiced individually. Whereas, spirituality is a personal set of beliefs and practices in developing the meaning and purpose of life and what you value in yourself. Individual spirituality is a personal quest for connection and enlightenment in our world. However, the spiritualist may also believe in a higher power. Though spirituality is an individual practice, it can easily be incorporated into religious habits as well. Each person's spiritual journey is unique. No two people answer questions in the same manner. Incidentally, both spirituality and religions enlighten our lives to gratitude. Gratitude enhances recovery from grief. It is the feelings of gratitude that will propel you forward on the road of restoration. Gratitude is a very important step in recovery but also for living an abundant life. There is more to look forward to than just getting past the pain.

Anyone of any religion or belief system has or will experience loss. Loss is painful. You must negotiate it to feel gratitude for having known this pet, person, or thing. The process graced you with what these things have taught you. However, you may have questioned why these painful losses entered your life and questioned when the pain will subside or disappear. You may also fight whether you might see your loved one again. You are not alone. If you did not contemplate life after death and the meaning of life before losing your loved one, now is the time. I cover "the meaning in life" more in chapter eleven. No matter what position you hold on the afterlife experience, you will know it is best to decide on your beliefs before encountering death to receive the most comfort.

I know this is a limited discussion on such a vast topic. I want you to understand my struggles and how I got through the tough emotions during grief. My discussion should clarify the subject of religion and spirituality, which can get muddled. Most importantly, know what they mean to you. Self-discovery and inner healing are your jobs, no one else's.

No one can answer life's questions for you. You must reach deep to find your answers. The very topic of living beyond this physical world takes time and contemplation. It is, however, one of the very subjects worth the effort. Reflecting upon one's life and death is hard. However, it is through life's certainties in one's beliefs and values that offer comfort during tougher times. Part of practicing religion or spirituality is knowing what you believe. This is how joy creeps in and peace covers you during adversity. You have also seen how a spiritual or religious attitude will aid you in enlightenment within yourselves and the world around you. Those seeking these insights are more prone to gratitude despite difficulties, which enhances recovery from loss. Since beliefs take a stand in finding meaning in our lives, it is a good time to dig deep and find the answers to your questions before life deals you another loss. Questions like: Why am I here? What is my purpose? How can I find the meaning to it all? It is those who live their lives fulfilled and grateful that come to the end of their lives with no regrets. They have asked and answered their own questions and lived intending to live out their beliefs.

You may choose religion, spirituality, or both to find your way in the world. I use both the religious and spiritual avenues of finding value and meaning in my life. I practice religion within a congregation but have a personal spiritual path as well. You can find meaning in your life after loss, which I will cover in chapter eleven. You are not yet ready for that part of your metamorphosis. (rebirth)

You can find relief and recovery from painful emotions, regardless if you have a pet. Everyone who has lived life will experience some loss and pain. Whether you are amid pain from a recent loss or have not recovered from past pain, you will find relief by going through the pain, not around it. Most won't know how to navigate that bumpy road of restoration from painful emotions. It is natural to feel a barrage of emotions after loss, but not natural to know how to maneuver those emotions. Anyone, regardless of religiosity, willing to get through the tough emotions and administer self-care will benefit. The important part of this chapter is knowing what you believe about life after death. The time you take to contemplate this issue will aid you in recovery.

*This is Lucky, another doggie friend who went to heaven*

## Points to consider:

- All the work you do towards understanding your beliefs will go a long way in recovering from grief.
- How you look at life's lessons, whether good or bad, is all perspective.
- You become participants in life rather than reactors when you know what you value.
- It will be your spiritual or religious attitudes that will aid you in enlightenment within yourselves and the world around you.
- Being aware of your beliefs and values will lead to gratitude rather than a feeling of lack in your life.
- Once you settle on your beliefs, you can find the meaning of your life.

Once you have taken the time to mull over what you believe, we can move on. You will learn more about yourself as you travel that emotional road. I plan to build upon your beliefs and add three other things to consider before we move to the process of grieving. Knowing what recovery, joy, and peace mean can add to the enjoyment of what you will have to look forward to beyond the sorrow of grief. You can mull over in your mind what you believe about these topics before reading, or jump in, read, and add to my explanations when you finish reading chapter four. They may mean many things to you. They may mean nothing amid the pain. Mainly, I want you to have these things to look forward to. There may be much pain and work between where you are now and where you will be after working through the grief process. You will come to understand those terms more in the upcoming chapter. You have much to look towards beyond your uncomfortable feelings.

> *"Death is not the greatest loss of life. The greatest loss is what dies inside us while we live."* ~Norman Cousins~

~~~

*"Recovery is a process. It takes time. It takes patience. It takes everything you got."~Author Unknown~*

# CHAPTER 4
## Recovery Peace Joy

We are broken when we face loss. It feels like all our pain, confusion, and disorientation are falling like a waterfall over a cliff crashing into the rocks below. Where we have been strong before, we are now weak. There is no understanding of our situation. Likewise, our brokenness is like a disease spreading all around us. Our pain affects everyone we have contact with. However, our resistance to the breaking process will only prolong it. At the same time, our willingness to yield to pain and growth will shorten our time in brokenness. Our brokenness is an opportunity to observe our lack of wholeness and spiritual maturity and respond to it. It can lead us to a place less judgmental and critical of ourselves and others. We are being refined like gold, skimming off impurities, (character defects) leaving the purist gold behind. We become humbled and refined, perfecting ourselves for usefulness and a better life ahead. This is the recovery process of grief. We mutate from brokenness to wholeness. There is light at the end of that long, dark tunnel.

> *"We learn more in our valley experiences than on our mountain tops."* ~Charles Stanley~

The process from brokenness to wholeness is the recovery process. It is inner healing. It's like taking lemons to make lemonade. The lemons themselves are sour or bitter. When we add sweetener and dilute it with water, we create a refreshing drink. The recovery process can be bitter, but the recovery of our joy and peace is sweet and refreshing. We do not have to be a slave to our bitter pain. Despite our sour situation, we can choose to squeeze the attributes we possess and are growing in and use them to become whole.

Adversity has a positive side besides making lemonade from lemons. The goal of adversity is to give life depth and value. Adversity pushes us beyond ourselves. It enlarges our purpose in life and equips us for that purpose. As a friend said, "You just added to your resume." Everything we learn through our trauma can help someone else going through similar adversity. We will be more useful in others' lives. And eventually, peace and joy will follow all that pain you thought would break you. We also learn through adversity the small irritants in life no longer matter. We can let adversity harden or soften our hearts. That response is our choice. Read Charles Stanley's *Advancing through Adversity* to find out more on the subject. It is a great adjunct to this book. Advancing through adversity takes one step at a time. Each step forward gets you closer to the complete picture.

We miss growth in our souls if, for some self-preserving reason, we oppose feelings in us that disturb us. What is problematic in our lives needs care and attention. However, it is easier to hide from emotions than to face ourselves. Dealing with the hidden truth will set us free. That freedom of facing ourselves is the freedom to be ourselves, with no excuses. The light of the truth may show some ugliness and imperfections we don't want to admit. However, our souls will always seek the light in the truth. You can hide, but that light will reveal your hiding place until it becomes too hard to ignore. We can never change or grow until we face the truth first. When this is your revelation, you are free to begin work in yourself toward recovery, transformation, wholeness, and usefulness. Look for pangs of emotions you don't recognize. They are revealing what is deep within your soul. They can result from the present loss or previous ones.

You may realize previous losses as you read *Floppy Ears*. There may be a pang of pain as emotions rise to the surface. My book opens your eyes to the losses you have endured in the past. I intend for you to inspect your life for all the losses never grieved. Deal with past emotions as they arise. It will aid in healing your present loss. It is healthy to grieve old losses. Only you will know if you have fully grieved the loss. As they appear in your memory or your heart, you will either feel intense pain, a dull ache, or even happiness if you have fully grieved and looked to the good you experienced in that relationship or other thing you lost. You will feel grateful for the time you shared with that pet, or person when you have overcome your loss.

Recovery, joy, and peace all encompass the process and result of self-care or soul care. *Care of the Soul* by Thomas Moore is an exhaustive book on the subject. Moore says the soul is the "dimension of experiencing life and ourselves". Every experience you encounter in life affects the soul. Your soul is how you present yourself, regardless of what has occurred in your life. I consider the soul, our mind, will, emotions, and personality. All who you are, come into play as you live your life and especially how you recover from grief. It behooves you to care for the soul and recover peace and joy.

*"Quit trying to be who you were and try being who you are now."* ~ Diana Lee~

## Recovery

Recovery is the portion of the book called "grief stages". *Dictionary.com* regards recovery as restoration to a normal state of health, mind, strength, or recovery of something lost or something gained. In other words, it signifies a problem one is attempting to fix. Recovery can mean many things to different people on their unique journey. Know that recovery is not to re-establish a pre-loss lifestyle. Your life will never be the same. But it can shift from hopeless to hopeful.

I prefer the ending of the definition, "something gained in recovery." Because I believe there is much to gain from loss. It won't feel like it yet. Every step will have challenges.

Work through it and you will feel differently. When you face challenges, you become stronger, as in my example of the weight lifter. The heavier the weight, the stronger you become. In addition, as one grows beyond the trauma, living becomes hopeful and satisfying, living for purpose and meaning in one's life. Recovery takes an adjustment to one's attitude, values, goals, and even the roles one plays in life. It is that positive outlook that increases functioning and emotional well-being. As you recover, you gain the ability to feel, think, and act in ways that enhance your enjoyment of life. Hope can rise from the ashes of sorrow. Joy will again creep in and a blanket of peace will eventually cover you in its warm embrace.

Keep in mind there is more than death people recover from; illness, grief from loss, domestic abuse, and mental illness, to name a few. Most think of recovery as associated with abstinence from drug and alcohol abuse. However, we can all use a recovery program to reclaim our lives after trauma. Recovery takes brokenness and trauma and turns them upside down. It is a process through which people improve in wellness. It can strengthen us. Enlightenment and upliftment of your spirit enable you to look forward again. You will learn the truth about yourself and that will set you free. What does recovery mean to you? Your definition might tell a different story from mine.

Recovery from grief has rewards because it teaches us many things about ourselves. For starters, it teaches us to accept help. That was a hard one for me. I can take care of myself, thank you. However, every day can be difficult, overwhelming, and just plain hard. Learn to accept help.

Let others who love you do things for you and don't be ashamed. We are all weak at some point in our lives and need others. We all need each other. Grief also teaches us perspectives we may never have noticed before. It causes us to consider our lives. We see what and who is important to us. What isn't? If you are taking others for granted, learn to appreciate those people. Most importantly, learn to love others and yourself despite imperfections. Allow yourself to learn about yourself and find all that is within.

Furthermore, during recovery, we will learn about emotions. We have many and some will be unexpected. They can debilitate and overwhelm us, causing us to not think properly or make sound decisions. I could not think straight for months after Danny died. I just wandered around, not knowing what I was doing or had done. Also, we are learning to identify emotions, which help in recovery. We will also learn to relate to others. You may not be the only one in your circle to lose what you have lost. Be supportive of others and assist them through the ordeal, too. You are vulnerable enough to understand their loss and offer support, encouragement, and empathy. Lastly, your faith may waver or grow stronger. It is up to you which way you choose to go. All these lessons learned cause us to adapt and develop aspects of our being—physical, mental, emotional, and spiritual that might have gone undeveloped had our trauma not occurred. We advance through it with deeper feelings of inner satisfaction with ourselves and with our lives. Our pain is never wasted when we learn from it.

Recovery is much like boot camp. I will not soften the blow. It is hard work, rigorous, painful, and challenging. It will take courage and fortitude to keep your balance. Perseverance and patience are required. Recovery does not happen overnight or more people would go through it. But recovery has rewards. Adversity enlarges our purpose in life. We advance through it with deeper feelings of inner satisfaction, coupled with what we learned. It may be a crazy rollercoaster ride, but exhilaration will carry you through to the next steep descent on the next truth. Buckle up.

Take that first step and then take only one step at a time. Don't get too caught up in the complete picture. You don't know what that picture looks like yet. The process can be overwhelming. Progress in small bite-sized achievements and celebrate each one. To stay persistent, note past persistence and recall and summon those same feelings of stubborn, unyielding, inspired, focused, committed behavior. Call on all of those feelings in your present pursuit. You must keep it up despite difficulties, delays, failure, or opposition from others. Don't give up. Be persistent even if it means you move ahead inch by inch. Not everything in life is a sprint. Any progress gives you the courage and faith to go on. However, you will need rest. Recovery is hard work, and you may have setbacks and resistance from yourself and others. Take care of your physical and emotional health so as not to burn out. No matter how persistent you are, take your time. You don't have to recover in a specific space of time, no matter what others think. This is not their journey. It is yours.

There is a story I read recently that illustrates what I mean by living through the pain. It's called:

## The Marble Statue

A marble statue stood in the middle of a large city surrounded by hundreds of marble tiles that visitors from all over the world stood on to admire the statue's beauty. One night, when the city square was empty, one of the marble tiles right in front of the statue spoke.

"Hey statue, don't you think it's unfair that people the world over come here to admire you while ignoring and stepping on me?"

The statue replied. "Don't you remember the sculptor actually cut us from the same block of marble?"

"Yes, I do! That's why it's even more unfair. Both of us came from that block, and yet the world treats you so differently now!"

The statue said, "Do you remember the day the sculptor tried to work on you, but you resisted his tools?"

"Yes, it hurt! I was mad at him! How could he use those nasty tools on me?"

The statue continued. "Well, because you resisted his tools, he couldn't work on you, so he decided to give up and work on me instead. I knew at once that I would be something different and unique after his efforts, so I bore all the painful tools he used on me and allowed him to craft me as he wanted."

The tile exclaimed, "But those tools were so painful!"

The statue said, "My brother, there is a price for everything in life. You resisted and gave up, so you can't blame anybody who steps on you now."

The marble tile silently listened to the statue's words and reflected on them.

~~~

You may stop reading and reflect on that story to gain the impact I intend for you. Then read on and discover the meaning of joy and peace.

~~~

*I call this joyful dog Max-a-Million. He is my good friends Bec and Stefen's dog.*

*He is the epitome of joy!*

## Joy

You may feel you will never feel joy or laugh again. When you do, it will shock you. It will creep up just that unexpectedly. I have met people who feel shame at laughing when a loved one has just passed. However, let no shame dampen the spirit of the soul, no matter when it bubbles to the surface. Joy is one of the most unexpected emotions during the grief journey and one you will welcome if you let it. Likewise, I want you to welcome all emotions. You don't have to act on them all, but recognizing them is the first step. Joy and sadness can coexist. I have felt both emotions simultaneously. I am not saying the same will happen to you. However, joy will be the break you need amidst all the sorrow. Let it flow. Be set free.

Joy is the emotional and mental state of well-being bubbling up from a well-cared-for soul. There will be feelings from calm delight to hilarity and every reaction in between. Joy is an intense, ecstatic feeling that surpasses all understanding in this turbulent world, full of pain. One cannot hide joy or its expression. Joy represents the character that lives deep within a person. A joyful person's face and surroundings illuminate with radiance. Their continence is different from an unjoyful person. However, not everyone feels joy. To me, joy is a gift. No one is responsible for or can steal your joy. Those who possess joy exude a positive, pleasant, and grateful attitude. They may laugh out loud, or find delight in success at any endeavor; at just meeting someone in the grocery store line to exchange pleasantries with. Joy gives us the strength to stand strong and keep going when life gets hard and we are overwhelmed, tired, or defeated by the weight of pain. Amid our trials, joy will bring endurance and strength to go on. Though there is a difference between joy and happiness. Both contain elevated feelings of well-being and delight. However, happiness depends on circumstances. I will be happy when this or that happens. Joy rises from the reservoir of our hearts and spirit despite circumstances, despite the loss. Enjoy life just as soon as you can after a personal loss and don't feel guilty about it. We mourn for another's loss because we no longer have them to love. However, there is much left to be grateful for that we can enjoy.

When we love others regardless of trials, we can feel the joy of love surrounding us. Likewise, we can recover joy when we give to others, even when it initially doesn't feel good. When I am going through my deepest sorrow, it helps to bring joy to someone else's life. Put aside your hurts and frustrations and give when you think you have nothing to give. Live for outreach, not in reach, and joy will find you! Someone may even bless you beyond what you gave. You can find relief despite your pain. Joy is the balm to soothe your soul. It comes from a well-cared-for soul. A well-tended soul allows gratitude, giving, joy, and contentment. Each step involved in healing gives us the feeling of renewal and refreshment. Joy is one of the most comfortable of emotions along with that cozy blanket of peace. Enjoy your life now, not later, when something good happens. Something good is happening right now if you look closer. If you don't find any good in your life, give something to someone and see joy rise in their life. It may seep into yours too.

Joy flows out of a grateful heart. Our joy depends much on our perspective and how we see our life. I think there is a deep well of joy within us. Some can tap into their joy while others have to work harder to bring it to the surface. In addition, we cannot enjoy life without gratitude. There is an abundance when you look. One can always find something to be grateful for, for all you are and all you have. Do not focus on what you do not have when you have so much. This kind of attitude might not come easily to some. It will have to be cultivated to become a steady part of your attitude. Gratitude is part of living intentionally. It is part of living in the now. Gratitude naturally follows a life that's lived in the moment because we don't miss what's right in front of us. What positive thing can you be grateful for right now? I have a gratitude journal where I list my abundance. Learn to live content in every and any situation and you will find joy!

Most of the time, I find joy in my gratitude for all God gives me. I find joy anytime I'm outside in God's creation, feeling the warmth of the sun on my skin, the wind ruffling my hair, and a simple leaf falling from a tree. I find joy in the creatures of the earth, both wild and free and domesticated. The sniff from the cold nose of a dog in my ear. There is joy in shushing down the steep slope on my skis, the snow-covered mountains in the distance, calling me to fresh adventures. I find joy in the soft skin of a baby and their trusting eyes. I find it in a friend's love and laughter, and remembrance of me in my trials. It's pure joy when I receive a call or text from someone I love. Joy is certainly in the love bursting from my heart and into another heart. I can find joy in the warmth of a crackling fire on a blustery day and the smells of food cooking in the kitchen and warm baked cookies. The laughter of friends filling my home. I find joy in the passing of scenes through the car window on a road trip and the stars and calls of the night. I find joy in learning something new; a foreign word, a new song on a keyboard, a revelation coming from a dream. A job well done, an organized closet and a clean house are what I find joy in. I find the most joy in doing something for others; a meal, a call, doing a kind thing, or an unexpected gift or card. I like to sing "Happy Birthday" even when it's not a person's birthday. There is joy in the new sprout of spring that I don't remember planting. I find joy in a good night's sleep! I'm betting you will find joy wherever you look for it too. Try it and see.

*"The deeper your sorrow carves into your being, the more joy you can contain." ~Kahlil Gibran~*

## Peace

Peace can seem as elusive as joy when you are mourning your loss, but you can find it if you look. As with all other feelings, peace is different for everyone. Where one finds peace, others find unrest. Peace does not mean there is nothing wrong with your life. But it is the opposite of emotional turmoil. Feeling peaceful is accepting the challenges in your life and still finding harmony, gratitude, and abundance. Peace is finding a stress-free state of security, safety, and calm. That calm comes from inside you, not outside. Peace fosters stability in many areas of your life—work, home, relationships, and finances, to name a few. When you have peace within you, all parts of your life flourishes.

There are many ways to combat a troubled soul and find peace. One can work out their emotions on paper through journaling as I have. Journaling, as I mentioned earlier, puts your feelings and life into perspective. You work out on paper what you might not figure out in your mind. Many emotions are bouncing around you when you face adversity. To be at peace, you accept those emotions. It is in accepting these feelings that give you the mindfulness of what is but also what can be. When we live intent on living and feeling those emotions, we are living in the moment. The unpleasant emotions will eventually pass and make room for the more pleasant feelings. You will learn more about how to handle your emotions in Chapter 5 in the section about "Becoming an emotional expert."

## Chapter 4

You know when you are in the presence of a person covered in peace. It shows not only in their lives but on their face and posture. Their health is usually good. You want to be around them, so some rubs off on you! Peace is a lovely emotion, sought after, but not always found. However, you will find peace in cleaning out the closet of your soul.

Why do some find peace when others don't? Everyone has challenges. No one escapes the trials of life. However, some cannot accept challenges, while others accept unrest, facing it with resilience. Resilience begins with your thinking. With emotions rolling around you, how do you pick which ones to allow into your mind and soul? It is first accepting all emotions and then choosing the ones most beneficial to your peace that make the difference. It is how you view yourself and your life. Loving acceptance of every part of your mental, physical, and emotional self creates contentment and peace inside you. You will learn more about acceptance in a later chapter.

Acceptance causes invaluable insight. It's allowing positive emotions and mindfulness of what is and what can be. Living in mindfulness and intentional living gives way to gratefulness because we don't miss what we would if our thoughts were on "what ifs." Savor the moment, the mood, and the experience, not in a hurry for the next thing. We are in way too big of a hurry these days. We are busy, busy, busy. Stop, and live for the moment, with who you are enjoying. Peace and joy are intentional options to take or avoid. However, peace is the wellspring of acceptance, which is the endpoint in the reality of your situation. Whichever comes first, joy, peace, and acceptance are of no importance. When we are grateful, we discover joy. When we accept our circumstances and live in the moment, peace evolves. Peace, joy, and acceptance create the merry-go-round that brings the most pleasure out of life.

*"Every day wasted is a day you will never get back."*
~Joyce Meyer~

## Mindfulness

Those who have peaceful countenances live with not only gratitude but intent and mindfulness. Dr. Justin Puder of the 14-day mindfulness course, says, *"Living mindfully is a non-judgmental awareness of the present."* This non-judgmental attitude is for others and yourself. This attitude of non-judgment allows peace to flourish. Peace accepts challenges and faces them with resilience. Go to the *Divethru* app, *"helping you go through what you're going through."* The doctor has online classes to help with everyday problems to the more excruciating issues. The *Divethru* website advocates deep breathing exercises, creative pursuits, meditation, and mindful journaling, including gratitude for the smallest blessings to find peace. I began to learn the keyboard amid my painful turmoil and find it takes my mind off my troubles, resulting in peace. Learning a new skill also gave me a sense of accomplishment, which helped towards a better attitude. I also use a gratitude journal to record what brings me joy in everyday life. This was my method of journaling at Danny's passing. He sure shone in my attitude of gratefulness. As with all our behaviors, it all begins with our thinking. Mary Kay, the cosmetic mogul, used to say, "What you think about, you bring about." Let it be something good.

When you are not taking your mind off your troubles through meditation, journaling, or mindful breathing, you can practice mindfulness instead. The idea is to live in the moment, the now, now, now. Mindfulness brings the present to the forefront without the past or future disrupting your thoughts. You label nothing, unlike when you labeled your feelings. Instead, you don't judge whether something is positive or negative. Let those judgmental thoughts be. You are simply enjoying the present moment to its fullest.

There are many mindful techniques to keep your mind from drifting. Mindful breathing is counting to four as you breathe in, hold four, let out four, and repeat. It is very relaxing and I do this multiple times a day. To practice mindful journaling versus journaling intending to empty feelings on paper, ask specific questions. How am I feeling at this moment? What do I notice in my surroundings? How can I accept today without judgment? What am I dwelling on presently? What do I want to focus on? Both types of journaling are beneficial to caring for your soul.

You can also practice mindful movement. This means a heavy, heart-pounding, sweaty, exercise or dance. For me, it's climbing the mountain behind my home without stopping. Focus on breathing, footfall, or the sun on your face. Be present with each body movement, weight lifted, or feelings in your muscles. This is an excellent way to leave your troubles behind, giving you the break from the emotional pain. Mindfulness takes your mind on vacation. Think back on how you arrived home from vacation; relaxed, refreshed, energetic, grateful, and in a positive state of mind. Vacation shows on your face and in your perspective. You are ready to face the world again. Use some techniques I outlined above. Take a few five-minute vacations throughout your day and experience the results of joy and peace. No one can put a price on that.

We may initially believe our loss has no value, only pain. However, our grief journey will call us back to what we value most in life. These are the intangibles in life, such as love, friendships, family, togetherness, contentment, beauty, health, joy, and peace. There are more important things than what we obtain and consume. I have already given you many techniques to recover joy and peace. However, you will find it in each step of the recovery process. Grief can lead to a fulfilled life with what matters most to you. However, these things take intentional attitudes and practices to recover or discover what you value most. When you compare what is happening to you versus what you think should happen to you, you gain insights into your character. You dig deep within your emotional well. The joy and peace you desire will arise out of the deep well of your soul. We can find more reasons to be joyful than sad. If we accept what is rather than what we'd like it to be, we find peace within that acceptance.

Points to consider:

- The process from brokenness to wholeness is the recovery process.
- You must go through the process. There is no shortcut, no matter how painful.
- The process will transform you into wholeness, maturity, and usefulness.
- You miss growth in your soul if you oppose feelings that disturb you.
- Recovery is hard work, rigorous, painful, and challenging.
- Recovery will take courage, fortitude, and perseverance.
- The result will be acceptance, joy, and peace.
- Joy is one of the most comfortable emotions, giving you the feeling of renewal and refreshment. Allow it.
- Loving acceptance of all your mental, physical, and emotional selves creates contentment and peace inside you.
- Use mindfulness to focus on and accept the process of recovery.

Even though I have warned you that the grief journey is hard and it will exhaust you, I hope I have given you enough to look forward to and you will join me on the journey. It will be a journey of valleys and mountaintops. The way around grief is through it. There is no other way. Recovery takes us from hopeless to hopeful, from broken to whole. Later in this book, the grief stages will take you through recovery one step at a time. However, it is important to know what those stages of grief represent. The following chapter will outline the stages and how you can become an emotional expert in them.

*"The only way to get to the other side is through the door."*
*~Helen Keller~*

~~~

*"Healing involves discomfort, but refusal to heal is infinitely more painful." ~Diana Lee~*

# Chapter 5
# What are Stages of Grief?

Now that you are aware of what viewpoint I stand upon, our desired outcome, and what keywords I will use, we can continue the discussion based on the professional's Stages of Grief. The stages of grief endow the reader with the idea of where they will tread on the grief journey, but also how incomplete recovery can affect relationships and capacity for happiness and peace.

There is no easy way around grief. It is through grief you find recovery and acceptance of what is. I have added my own stages to the professional stages as I went through the grief process, first with my pupster and then when my fiancé died. If it helps you through grief, add anything you want that may help. You will learn as you pass through the stages what you are feeling and how to deal with the agony and other emotions. You will also discover what is normal for you is not normal for others. Keep your eyes on yourself and your recovery. Take each stage slowly and move on when you feel comfortable with yourself. You will discover subtle peace when you are ready to move to the next part of the process. You already know how painful loss can feel. Be gentle with yourself, but keep progressing. You will feel better in small ways a little at a time. However, you will arrive through the door of restoration, I promise.

The stages of grief will transform you. If you are in the midst of pain or have experienced loss before, you cannot imagine some prescribed format will ease the suffering and desolation. The wound of loss feels like you are in deep water with the level up to your nose and if you move or breathe, you will drown. You ask yourself how following this map of bereavement will transform you from immeasurable sorrow to peace and joy, as I have promised. If you have followed some new diet fad that your best friend lost ten pounds on, only to discover this plan did not work for you, you may wonder, "How can a prescribed set of standards on grief work for me?" You saw how this great diet plan worked for your friend, but not for you. How are these stages of grief different?

First, the stages of grief are highly individualized. The stages are not positions you tick off a list. Then, when you complete the list, you become healed of all the emotions surrounding your grief. Grief will come and go. It doesn't disappear forever like catching a cold and getting well. These stages are reactions you may go through in response to your loss. Not everyone responds the same and consequently may not go through each stage or, conversely, breeze through on the way to another step. Each phase is a framework to identify feelings you may be perceiving. The entire process helps you make sense of your pain and how you will deal with it all. Know you will realize your total loss when you can deal appropriately with individual emotions. When you feel at ease in one step, you are ready to move on to the next, even if you have to return to any steps. It's all okay in the scheme of healing. Trust the process and keep taking one step at a time. Navigate the steps at your own pace in your way. It is more a process than a set of steps.

*Floppy Ears* is based on the stages of grief produced by professional counselors. Some do not consider Elisabeth Kubler-Ross, a Swiss-American psychiatrist, the original developer of the five stages of grief. However, her model for grieving has been the most followed over the years. She permitted us to grieve. She did not advocate stuffing the pain deep inside. Elisabeth offered us a healthy avenue to experience a transformation from deep sorrow toward peace. This psychiatrist and author provided the stages of grief for terminally ill patients and later saw how they worked for those grieving loss, too. The Swiss-American psychiatrist coined the model for grief in 1969, which has become the most widely known form of healing.

However, "Incomplete recovery from grief can have a lifelong negative effect on the capacity for happiness," says John W. James and Russell Friedman, who wrote *The Grief Recovery Handbook*. "Grief can crush, like the weight of a thousand pounds pressing against your heart." The grieving process can be overwhelming, with too much coming at you all at once. No one can tell you how to do it perfectly, but if you know the general process of grief, it can help you identify what you are going through. When you understand where you are, you know better how to handle it, and where you are heading on that journey. Grieving is the vehicle in which you recover from your losses.

The five stages of grief are; denial, anger, bargaining, depression, and acceptance. However, your initial grieving will probably be feelings of denial and anger. I cover each stage in separate chapters. One doesn't progress through each stage in a linear order. You may skip around, come back around, go through some steps more than once, skip steps, or be in more than one stage. Everyone is different and will handle pain personally. If someone doesn't cry initially, they may still be in denial, and it may come later. Or maybe they feel they will never stop crying once they start. Don't judge how others go through their pain. It is a personal experience. Grief has its timing in each individual.

Grief is more than pain. It is a wound so deep that you may first become numb and empty so you don't have to experience the pain. You try to feel nothing because a full-frontal assault of the excruciating pain will surely kill you. Your world has stopped, but the clock ticks on. After the numbness subsides, unexpected feelings of all sorts rise to the surface above the pain. There is a mixture of conflicting emotions, anger, unforgiveness, guilt, relief, and even peace, depending on your circumstances. These deep wells of emotions are confusing and hard to separate and decipher. It is because deep sadness is such a hard emotion to hang on to for any length of time that other emotions bring relief. You are in the middle of coping with uncertainties and the chaos of emotions. You don't know what to do with them all. Most people don't know what's normal in grief even if they experienced loss. What's normal to one is not normal to the next person. We cannot gauge the truth of our situation through our emotions until we can separate and address them. Through the recovery process, you will become an emotional expert.

*"I am certain that learning to recognize and execute emotions will make your world a better place to live." ~Diana Lee~*

## Becoming an emotional expert

It's important to become an emotional expert while going through the grief process. It will also be important to find the tools to recognize and manage your emotions. I have given you that tool in the next paragraph. Accept that grief can trigger many different and unexpected emotions. Some you may not have experienced before. I found an online "mood tracker" app that will help you find the emotions you are experiencing and then deal with them. You can download The Mood Tracker on your phone to refer to anywhere, anytime. You will learn to identify, work through, and self-regulate your emotions through this tool.

First, the Mood Tracker tells us to validate our emotions. Give yourself permission to feel them without changing that emotion to an "acceptable emotion", or worse yet, burying the feelings. Put a name on that emotion. How are you feeling today or at this moment? Do you know? Check out their helpful chart of faces pinpointing what you are feeling on the "Mood Tracker" app if you don't know. We use the same "faces" printout with alcoholics and drug addict clients who don't know what they feel but can choose a face on the page to match their mood. They drink and consume drugs to hide the feelings they can't identify or deal with.

After pinpointing your mood or emotion, follow the next step. Feel the emotion. Accept it, observe it, allow it. It is okay to have emotions. That makes us human. This approach is the important transition from what is healthy or doing something harmful to yourself. Ignoring or stuffing emotions will not get you through your grief. Some emotions you experience may surprise you, but focusing on that emotions will get you started on the road to healing. I listed some emotions below for reference. You can find the "faces" mood chart at the back of the book.

*Sad, frustrated, angry, hopeful, afraid, happy, smug, jealous, disgusted, confused, guilty, surprised, lonely, depressed, ecstatic, worried, ashamed, embarrassed, distracted, hopeless, empty, confident, nervous, enraged, exhausted, proud, cautious, guarded, shocked, overwhelmed, shy*

After emotion identification, it is important to know what triggered the emotion in your soul. When you know your triggers, you can avoid them. If you can't avoid it or need to experience that emotion, get through it. Only after you live through the emotion can you choose to respond with dignity. It is also important to know that these emotions aren't permanent. They will pass and other emotions more comfortable will take their place.

The next step in your emotional expertise is to share what you are feeling instead of making others around you uncomfortable. Don't say, "nothing's wrong," if indeed you feel sad. Communicate authentically. Others will also be more inclined to share with you when you contribute first. Talk about it, or journal, and do not let your emotions ruin your day. Accept all your soul offers and be good to yourself. Emotions can exhaust you. Take time during the process. It is extremely important to share only with those who have your best interests at heart and will not judge you. Get into a group of those with shared interests and know your pain. Or share with a friend or family member who has experienced such sorrow. In time, you will become an emotional expert. It takes practice, but later it will become second nature.

It was in journaling I learned about getting through my grief and how to guide you. My journal takes you through my process, but know it will not be your manner of handling suffering. We all bear pain differently, depending on our temperaments and personalities. How we handle change can determine how we grasp the loss. How we suffer can also depend on how and when the person or pet died. Was it sudden or long and drawn out? It also depends on how long and how close we were to the one we lost. No matter the circumstances, you can deal with all grief. There is no right or wrong way to grieve. There are as many ways to grieve as there are people in this world. Every individual will learn what is pertinent to their character, growth, and maturity needed. I have given you techniques for working through your emotions as you traverse the process. You know how to recognize emotions and triggers as they arise. You can't ignore feelings when becoming an emotional expert, but must accept them. I am also certain that learning to recognize and execute emotions will make your world a better place to live. For this moment, it is all about you and your recovery. Know that later, your recovery will be about others.

*Summer–Bec and Stefen's dog*

## Points to consider:

- The stages are reactions you may go through in response to your loss.
- When you feel at ease in one step, you are ready to move on to the next stage.

- The five professional stages of grief are denial, anger, bargaining, depression, and acceptance.
- I added the *meaning of life* and *what I love about you* to the stages for complete recovery.
- You will identify, validate, and feel the emotions before accepting and using them for growth.
- Incomplete recovery from grief can have a lifelong negative effect on the capacity for happiness and peace. It will also negatively affect your relationships.
- Journaling is an excellent avenue to process all you are feeling and what triggers the emotion.

The next chapter takes you through the first stage of grief. All the stages will be easier now that you know how to navigate your emotions.

*"Don't ask for a blessing—be a blessing." ~Diana Lee~*

~~~

*"Denial is the door she slams in her own face, trapping her in this lonely comfort zone. It keeps her from facing what hurts.*
*~Judith Sills~*

# CHAPTER 6
## Stage One—Denial

This isn't something you want to hear, but mourning is a very self-centered process. Self-pity is selfishness, a trap that keeps you in pain. Pity may comfort for a time, but it isn't powerful. It does not allow outward concern for others, only concern for your own needs. Know that my every intention is for you to rise eventually above the pain to arrive at an emphatic, compassionate place in your heart. If you stay in self-pity over your loss or situation, you will not rise above it enough to bring compassion and comfort to those in your life who need it for their recovery. This book differs from other books in its direction of overcoming grief. It is not just about you. My ultimate purpose for you is to be others-centered and to learn how to minister to others in your life who matter. The refining results of pain are perfecting us for usefulness in this world. There will always be someone worse off than you. Stop blaming others for your junk. Take responsibility for your healing. Help others instead of wallowing in self-pity. You will get better faster. However, you will go through more than your share of grief and pain before you arrive at your usefulness to humanity. Life is the largest self-help program designed for man.

*"The pit is the beginning of a pity party. Don't stay there."*
*~Diana Lee~*

*"Compassion opens the door to patience, kindness, generosity, and actions rooted in love."* *~Charles Stanley~*

Now, let's get to the steps and begin our healing.

## Stage One Denial

The first stage of grief we may experience is denial. There may be shock and numbness, mainly when a death occurs suddenly or while someone is away from home when they pass. One wants to deny their loved one is gone but coming through that door any minute. You may hear someone say, "I just can't believe they're gone." They can believe their loved one is gone, but their mind can't let the emotional rage inside come to the surface. Denial is not pretending the pet or person isn't gone. They just can't live with the reality of all the turmoil inside. It would be too many feelings at once. People may be in shock or feel fearful of living without such a supporting character in their lives. They may feel dazed, not knowing what is next for them, the great unknown. They

# Chapter 6

may get busy with all there is to do with arrangements and altogether avoid any emotion, burying the barrage lying in wait to pounce upon them. At this stage, one doesn't want to understand the whole situation and all the ramifications. You couldn't handle it. Survival is all you can think about. You wish to wake up in the morning with them waiting for you in the kitchen.

I feel as though my first stage of grief was incessant crying. I went to sleep crying and woke up with tears on my pillow. Even sleep knew my pain. Tears would start falling down my face while not thinking of my pain, but doing everyday chores. I was afraid to go anywhere, fearing the tears would fall and make someone uncomfortable. It seemed I cried for months without end. I thought I would never stop crying. This is not a stage of grief, but overwhelming sadness predominated my every move. I don't think I felt anything else but pain.

If anyone has given thought to life, we know death will follow. We will all cross over from life to death at some point. One reason I start my book with the acceptance of death and how you feel about life after death is because death is inevitable. Saying goodbye is not what we think about when we take our pets into our homes and hearts, but in reality, we will lose them someday, and grieving will begin. Anyone we love can leave at any time. They don't have to be ill or old. My fiancé was only sixty-one years old. Our life was just beginning. Someone asked me if I would rather have had Danny die before our wedding, as he did, or after our day of vows and celebration. Hands down, I would choose to have our day to celebrate our love and make memories.

Love is the only thing we take with us into eternity. I choose to take all of it I can with me when I go. Pain and joy are equal in the scheme of living and learning, Both hold equal value in the scheme of recovery. One cannot live one without the other.

Here is my first day without my pupster and how I didn't want to go to sleep for fear I would wake up and he would be gone. This is a good example of denial.

*I woke the following morning in tears. My dreams did not let me forget my experience the night before. I have this saying, "The heart never forgets, even when our memories fail us." We may want to forget about our loss as though it were only a dream. We may want to wake up and believe it was all untrue, a mistake. However, our hearts have known love and loss. It remembers all those complex emotions, even when our brains want to forget, even when our mind wants to remember. Our hearts will never forget what we have lived and known.*

Perhaps we don't even want to wake up. How can we face a day without our loved one? There is much to do? How can we look upon the life we lived with their belongings staring back at us, reminding us we once had a life, and now we don't? It is like we both acted a part in a play; you are playing your role, but where are they to play theirs? For Paddy and me, it was a dance.

*We were a dance, him and me. Some people might call it a routine. I labeled it a dance. We were not always in step, and I would trip over him and step on his toes, but eventually, it looked like a syncopated step, practiced until perfect. We both knew where the other was and moved according to the space they occupied. Both knew the next interchange. We moved apart and back together, heart to heart. Now I have only my memory of my dance partner. I suppose long-time married couples have that same in-sync step through life, each knowing what to expect in the other.*

*Paddy began each morning looking to me for direction. "Which dance are we going to do?" he seemed to say; the cha-cha, the waltz, the rumba, the dance of love? "No, silly boy, we will brush your teeth and brush your hair smooth before you can dance. You want to smell fresh with your black spots shiny before you present yourself, don't you?" He was always at the door to the bathroom while I showered. He would enter the shower with me without coaxing, ready for his bath. I would hold him under the spray and let the warm water fall across his back and head, softly washing away the trail's dust and some spot of grease he acquired beneath my car. When he was ready to present himself clean and fresh, I called him "the city puppy." He particularly liked his blow-dry. He patiently waited while I blew him dry and fluffed his fur. Then he would run out the door and roll around the floor in pure joy. I feel like that sometimes after a shower, though I never frolic as he does. I don't know why not.*

**The morning after and how comfort from friends makes a difference. Your friends and family will mostly be there for you in the beginning. They might expect you to "move on" at a later point. Get all the comfort you can now.**

*My understanding friends have been here all morning for me. I read in my bible II Corinthians 1:3-7 how God takes us through all things with comfort. Even when we are heavy with troubles, He is merciful in bringing relief. We can, in turn, offer others the same support God gave us. I can only imagine the pain so many have experienced in their lives; those who have lost children, spouses, or parents who didn't have the chance to raise their children. My hope in all this pain is to console others someday, the comfort God has given me through good friends and family. I heard Tony Evans say that our horizontal relationship with others in providing soothing relief, directs a vertical path into heaven and God. It can only strengthen our relationship with Him. He shows us how to love and cheer others. He then pushes us forward to replicate His love and the arms of comfort. We are ready even when we don't know it yet, just by going through grief and receiving relief. I wish giving and receiving comfort would be the way of the world.*

When others wrap us in comfort, we are better able to deal with the pain. There may very well be fear mixed in your cocktail of emotions. We hardly know what to do without our loved one. They aren't waiting for us in the kitchen the following morning. Their belongings are there, but they are nowhere around. We don't know what we will do without them, and yet there are still things to be done. Now there is more to do than ever, with funeral and memorial arrangements, company underfoot, well-wishers and obituaries, and, and, and... the list goes on. How can I ever get through this, you ponder?

Even after days of crying, I was not ready to release the things belonging to Paddy. I was not prepared for that much reality.

*I am ready to burn the pile of tissues I have thrown in Paddy's bed and maybe put his blanket back, perhaps, but then again, maybe not. No, I am not ready to release his blanket from my clutches. It still smells enough of him to hang on one more day or two. Though each day it smells more like me, our scents mingled into one, like us becoming one. We were one, and one without the other was not the same creature. I will forever be someone new in having known Paddy.*

## Chapter 6

The reality of work finally rose its ugly head to make me face my life. We are a productive society, expected to go forth and return to our work and lives after losing a loved one. Though this is not always easy, it is what we eventually do. Some like to work sooner to find some normalcy occupying themselves with work rather than suffering, looking outward instead of looking in. Looking within ourselves is scary and painful. We may put off feeling our emotions, our sorrow, our rage, and our pain as long as we possibly can. Eventually, those feelings will bubble to the top and come out unexpectedly. Yet others will hang on to the pain as if it is a lifeline. If agony is the only emotion that attaches us to our loved one, we will hang on with white knuckles, not wanting to let go into the unknown.

*I went to work today. It was time to quit crying, at least temporarily. I made cookies so I would have something to give others. When I'm hurting and need comfort, it makes me feel better to give back to the world what others need. Providing love and relief for others eases the pain, similar to a balm over a wound. I have not figured out how this occurs, but I discovered this phenomenon years ago, and it works every time.*

*I still have not told my employer about Paddy's death. She often asks about Paddy's welfare, but I don't want to share with her yet and pray she does not ask. However, I have been informing my neighbors when they see me walking and hiking about our hills, so they will already know about Paddy and not ask about his whereabouts. I would rather be the one to tell them rather than respond to their questions. There is something wrong if your pet is not with you when you are out and about. I ran into Peter, a neighbor on my way over to watch Brodie, another dog. He was walking* their dog, Tara. They call her Patches, even though her name is Tara because a bobcat snatched her on a walk one night and tore her up pretty bad. Tara is still young and vibrant. Peter takes the news about Paddy with grace and compassion. He has lost many dogs over the years I have known him. Our neighbors all know each other through each other's dogs. Everyone knew Paddy. They also know he had a good sixteen years and knew he never suffered. "Paddy had a good life," they would say. Yes, Paddy had a good life, and he made my life a good life too.

Getting out of the house forced me to face reality and my denial. Talking about your loss makes it more real. I later encountered the perfect example of someone in denial years after her son's and husband's death.

I know a woman who lost her son and then her husband in the space of one year. She still asks every day, "Where's Mike?" Every day she looks for her husband. She knows deep in her soul that her loved ones are gone. There was this look on her face after asking about them or looking for her mate and stating what she knows in her heart. They are gone forever. She has been doing this for an entire year. I hope she will move beyond denial soon. She is a vital woman, able to live a robust life with family and friends who love her. She simply cannot let out all the pain within her. It would be too much for her to handle. The incomplete recovery from her loss is keeping her from fully living. We don't think of living initially after loss. Instead, we think more about getting through each moment. Denial will wind down eventually. We see reality one step at a time, probably the only way we can handle grief.

## Chapter 6

Knowing the stages of grief is not enough. Even if we don't go through each stage, we have to go through the process. We only go through the steps necessary for our relief and recovery. Each step of grief transforms us into someone new. The complete process becomes not who we lost from our life, but the life we have lived with them. It's who we have become, knowing them, and who we are becoming without them. Once we get past the denial, the sooner we will allow other emotions in so they can do their work. Again, don't hurry the process, just stay the course and let others comfort you while they are there. Eventually, most people go away, back to their lives.

*Many people call and text their empathy and love over the loss of my best buddy of almost sixteen years. It warms my heart, fills my hours, and occupies my days to not fall into despair or loneliness. I try to balance my time with things that need attending but remembering the remarkable life we shared, and taking the time to grieve.*

It will be very important to take the time to feel the emotions you are experiencing. Denial is ignoring all within you so you can survive the pain. Once you have felt the pain, the anger, the grace, and forgiveness, you can see more of what life is all about. You will indeed live the life you wouldn't accept when you first lost your loved one. You are moving past the denial stage when the emotions rise to the surface. I felt denial way into my recovery from grief, but I didn't stay there.

You may have felt many emotions initially — pain, numbness, disbelief, and denial. Each day is a challenge to wake up to the reality of your loss. Start by letting others help and comfort you. Talk to someone you trust not to judge your pain or decisions. But do not make any life-altering decisions either. You are not healthy enough to make wise choices. Only make the ones needed right now. Go back to work if you have to, but not to avoid the pain. You need to work through the discomfort. If you bury the uncomfortable feelings, they may pop up at some inconvenient time. Only work if you need to follow your normal habits to feel better. Stay home if you can and engage in other normal habits. You may not want to open your eyes in the morning to face the day. But get up, have your tea or coffee, shower, make your bed, whatever is normal for you. The key is to let the emotions flow, no matter what you choose to do or not do. Feelings can be unpredictable and unreliable. You may feel one way one day and another way the next. It can be crazy-making. You will learn to decipher and separate the mix of emotions arising all at once.

## Points to consider:

- Mourning is a self-centered process that keeps you powerless when you stay there. The refining results of pain are perfecting you for usefulness in this world.

## Stage 1—Denial
## Characteristics:

- Dreamlike state and fear
- Pain
- Survival mode

- Shock and numbness
- Confusion and disbelief

## Possible action to take:

- You can continue to ask yourself the inevitable questions. The answers will bring the denial to the surface so you can face reality.
- You can also surround yourself with those who listen and bring you comfort, without advice or judgment.
- Give yourself time alone to feel your sorrow.
- Don't make any life-altering decisions.
- Get up and get on with your living habits to feel some normalcy.
- Write in your journal. List what you are and aren't in control of.

## Question to ask yourself:

- Could you really have prevented their death? Are you in control of anything that happens, such as death? The only thing you can control is your response.

The next grief stage is anger. It may feel uncomfortable, however, it may feel good to feel something other than the pain. Anger may not be a way you express yourself normally, but these are not normal times. Accept anger as part of the process you may go through to heal.

~~

*"When you feel dog tired at night, it may be because you growled all day."*
*~Anonymous~*

~~

*"Anger is the calling card no one wants to accept." ~Diana Lee~*

# CHAPTER 7
## Stage Two—Anger

Besides the pain in grieving, there can be anger and rage too. It seems if we succumb to sadness, we may drown in our tears, in the murkiness of our emotions, submerged in darkness and the unknown. For some, anger will be more acceptable than feeling pain. We can push people away by raging about our loss. Then they will leave us alone to drown in our misery. We may feel safer in our anger than in our sorrow. We can stand above the pain as on a rock, and agony can't touch us as long as we stay angry. Anger may not be our usual way of exhibiting frustration—however, we are not in typical times. We can't expect ourselves to act normally. Never expect anger to be logical in times of grief. It may cause you to feel guilt and shame. But give yourself the grace you would extend to those you love. Keep moving ahead in this chapter and I will teach you to deal with anger.

Some people may make you angry when they are trying to comfort you. They may say well-meaning things such as, "you have to move on sometime. Get into a grief group. You need to get rid of their belongings, move out of that big house," or my favorite, "it was just a pet. You can get another dog." Not everyone in our circle of friends and family has the capacity to understand our pain or anger. Your loved ones won't always say the right things. They may not know how to act and will say they know how you feel. They don't understand or know how you feel, and it makes you mad! However, beneath all that rage is pain, waiting to show its face. There is unrelenting pain and sorrow just below the surface. Understand that anger is a ruse to cover you for the moment until you can deal with the ache within you.

Some offered comfort, and it felt good. Then some tried to comfort me in their way but only made me mad.

*I am thankful today for those who have hung in with me in my pain, recognizing it will not vanish so quickly. I will still need comfort in the days to come. Sympathy cards arrived in my mail, one from the hospital where Paddy died. They see pain every day. How compassionate they must be to go on day after day looking into the face of suffering and death, yet able to give continual love and compassion. Death has taught me that much. However, not everyone can understand the loss of a pet.*

It is not wise at this point to share with those who will not have compassion for what pain you must be experiencing. They will only hurt you more or make you angry unless they are teachable. Some people need to learn to comfort others. Children usually never grasp comforting others if they weren't consoled growing up. The past is significant here. Its experiences draw the map of how we respond in adulthood. Not that those people don't have compassion. They might possess the heart to hurt for you. They

## CHAPTER 7

*crave comfort themselves, but the ability to make others feel better escapes them. The most genuine emotional connections arise from being or giving support. It is essential to the human bond. It is so simple that a child could learn. However, not everyone does.*

*Comfort comes in all forms, like my friend who calls every day, twice a day, asking how I'm doing, bringing wood, and asking for cookies, because he knows it brings me comfort to be kind. It can also be soothing words, cards, and U-tubes on pet loss, but mostly it is listening as we spill our grief into your lap and tell of our death experience, the daily pain of our loss, and the constant ruminations of life with our pet. It may be the repeating of stories one has already heard. Listening to your friend in their grief is the highest form of comfort. If you are the one to comfort another in their loss, just listen. Ask a few questions to keep them going, and then, you got it, just listen.*

*The process of grief is different for everyone. Some people will not be ready to speak about their experiences. Give them time. For me, it is going over and over in my mind the things I know of death, the things I'm learning about death. It is also trying to remember and not lose the memories that kept me going for all the years through my trials. As I held Paddy for the last time, his limbs quivering, I knew he had given me so much more than I had ever given him. I learned to love unconditionally, loving others as he loved me without expecting love in return. I had such a heart filled with love that it might burst if I did not give some away, and so I did.*

Knowing I still had love inside me was a relief. My love did not die with the one I had loved. I could still feel love. That was my first step in knowing I might be okay. I could also find a life outside of my grief and loss. Even though there was anger, I knew it was the stepping stone to relief. Now it is time to understand our anger more fully and learn to deal with it. We will need perseverance, patience, and kindness to serve us in managing our anger. Following are the steps to take from a website called *Good Therapy* in an article called, "From sad to mad: how suppressing your sadness invites anger," by Joshua Nash LPC-C April 15, 2014.

## Understanding the nature of anger.

Overcoming anger is a process, just as recognizing emotions, finding joy, and peace and acceptance are steps to recovery. First, one must understand the type of anger we have. Because there are two kinds of anger, you must approach them in different ways. There is righteous anger felt as an injustice in our world, then anger as the secondary emotion. When we go through loss and grief, and experience anger, we are displaying the secondary type of anger. One must fully accept or feel the primary underlying emotion. We judge the primary emotion as physically uncomfortable or feel a stigma towards it, suppressing its full expression. Consequently, we display a more acceptable emotion, anger. As I expressed before, anger will hold us above the pain so that we don't have to feel excruciating distress. Sadness, guilt, anxiety, and fear are the primary emotions that get transformed into anger. Sadness is the one we are most concerned with here, but you may feel a mix of other feelings as well. When I see an angry person, I give them the benefit of the doubt that what I don't see might be overwhelming sadness. This attitude keeps me from reacting to their anger.

Joshua from the website, Good Therapy, informs us it is through feeling the genuine emotion behind anger we allow ourselves to honor what we lost. Not feeling our sadness prevents us from accessing the importance of the thing we lost. When we can't engage with our sadness, we lose access to the memories and everything we honor in them. Conversely, by re-engaging in life, and inquiring into our sadness, in kind curiosity, we find exactly what we miss in what we lost. You can recover from your anger by following these steps.

## Steps to recover from anger.

1. When you feel angry, stop and sit down. Feel the energy inside you. Instead of showing outward signs of anger, take stock of where you are holding it in your body. That energy will subside as you focus on where you feel it. Now ask yourself a couple of questions. One, what are you feeling? This may be obvious, but if you take your time to answer honestly, your answer may surprise you. The second question to ask yourself is, why am I feeling sad, fearful, anxious, or guilty, whichever the case may be? Again, you may feel the answer is obvious, but give yourself a chance to answer and see what develops. While you thought you were angry, you might discover some other emotion needing to be addressed.

2. Once you have accessed your feelings and the emotion is sadness, it's time to feel the pain. Grumble, grumble, here we go again, back to sadness, the emo-

tion you were trying to avoid all along. Go back to chapter 4 under the subtitle, "becoming an emotional expert" to refresh your memory on how to pinpoint what emotions you are feeling if you need to. The main point is to acknowledge the emotion and name it. Feeling sad is uncomfortable and why we cover it with anger. Joshua had a trick he uses in accepting sadness as the emotion we need to deal with. Say out loud, to yourself, "yes," or just nod your head in the affirmative. He claims this trick makes emotion easier to access. Now, instead of anger, you feel sadness. Now what?

3. Sit there and feel your sadness. That emotion will lose its intensity in time. The next step is to inquire into what you lost, not so much what or who, but what those things represent. What is it you value in what you lost? Were they your supporting partner, did you lose a sense of fairness, loss of independence, loss of control, or do you miss the kindness that person represented? We often become angry when we don't experience our core values anymore, as expected. It will take patience and persistence to sit still and feel and do an honest assessment to arrive at that missing value. You may never have considered what you value in that person or pet. This is good practice for appreciating relationships, which I will address later in the book.

4. Now that you know what is missing, go out into the world and cultivate elsewhere what quality (what you value) went missing in losing your loved one. I

## Chapter 7

missed my pupster's unconditional love and sought those who loved me no matter what. In Danny, I missed his kind heart. I then sought those who were kind to me. Of course, I still missed them both, but what I value in my life with them, I looked for elsewhere.

This step explains why I am generous and intentionally kind when I experience loss. I make cookies or help someone organize. I use my gifts to bless others because it's those acts of kindness and generosity I miss so much in my fiancé, Danny. You may also forgive and behave gently towards others who need it because you value and need those qualities while you are mourning. Doing for others gives you a sense of control and power over your uncontrolled situation. You may even feel a positive sense of accomplishment, which you can carry into other areas of your life to help you move forward.

Anger has a sense of powerlessness that can make you even angrier. Doing these steps to identify emotions and deal with them will give your power back. Once you gain your sense of power and control, peace will follow. I have warned you that all these techniques will take time, persistence, and work. The reward is further understanding yourself. Peace will seep in little by little. Keep up the good work. These techniques take practice and maybe a change of attitude. But I promised you transformation, joy, and peace as long as you will transcend your challenges, objections, doubts, gripes, and reluctance. Then all these things will be added to your life. Just do it and peace will follow.

*"If what we are doing with our anger is not achieving the desired result, it would seem logical to try something different."*
~Harriet Lerner~

Letting go of your anger will clear your mind and help you view the one you loved more distinctly, the love, the fun, the adventures you shared. When you move into this precise idea of what you possessed for such a time, you realize and appreciate what they offered you, what they taught you, and what they meant to you. Your grief is more apparent and direct. Your grieving is more focused. You know you are moving towards recovery. Sadness or anger may still be present, but you're learning skills that will forever change your life for the better, regardless of your loss. Controlling your anger becomes easier as you understand it more. Don't feed it. Starve it until it is no longer anger, but the genuine emotion beneath the surface. You can deal with that emotion instead.

Anger is a powerful emotion. If you don't get to the root cause of it, it can fuel resentment and a bitter root. As I have said before, if one lets emotions settle deep inside your soul without dealing with them, they fester like an infection. You could be rude or mean to someone for no reason. These resentments can affect relationships and communication. Many times, the anger can boil over into rage that hurts everyone involved. Quick-tempered people often behave foolishly and cause themselves harm. Sometimes they hurt people and sometimes objects. If there is damage, it needs to be repaired. In contrast, dealing with the underlying emotions results in understanding, demonstrating wisdom, and restraint. Your soul will be at peace as anger dissipates. You will be at peace.

*"If you are patient in one moment of anger, you will escape a hundred days of sorrow."* ~Chinese proverb~

You have gained a good many skills at this point. However, we have another skill to learn under the banner of anger—unforgiveness. Anger frequently covers unforgiveness. There are signs you hold unforgiveness in your heart. Often, you exhibit an angry outburst at anyone at hand, not always the person you are angry with. Conversely, you may throw around snide remarks to the offender. Or you become compulsive to feel in control. You can literally make yourself ill over unforgiveness. These are only some signs of unforgiveness. This is too large of a topic to cover here. Know that no one is responsible for your feelings. No one can make you mad, sad, or angry. Emotional maturity is knowing you alone are responsible for your happiness and peace.

*"Anger makes you smaller, while forgiveness forces you to grow beyond what you were."* ~Cherie Carter Scott~

If you are unsure whether unforgiveness is a problem, ask yourself these questions:

1. Is it possible I replay scenes in my mind of someone who has disappointed or hurt me intentionally or in their ignorance?

2. Do I really want the best for the person who hurt me?
3. Or do I want that person to hurt as much as I hurt?
4. Is this anger I feel possibly at myself?

If you answered yes to any of these questions, you are probably living in unforgiveness. You need a good book to deal with those feelings. Unforgiveness is a heavy load to carry through life. It is like many uncomfortable feelings— the more you ignore them, the more unsettled your life will be. Less peace and joy will fill your days. You hurt no one but yourself when you don't forgive. That other person goes on blissfully with their life. Forgiveness is for your freedom. Overall, you must forgive yourself.

Forgiveness is part of letting go of your anger. You realize you are angry with the one who died. You are mad about the stupid things people say. Perhaps you feel agitated with yourself for not doing or saying what you could have when you had the chance. However, I believe it is never too late to forgive yourself and others. Sometimes it's harder to forgive ourselves over another. However, one can accomplish anything they set out to do if determined enough. When you practice forgiveness and grace, you feel more alive. When you have dealt with unbidden emotions, it is finally a relief to control those feelings and choose your actions. Taking that step towards and through forgiveness is one step closer to ease and comfort. Take time to forgive those who have hurt you. It may take more time than you think. Live with no regrets.

Besides, you can still talk to your loved one or the one who has hurt you. Tell your loved one you are furious at them for preceding you in death, leaving you alone to deal with life. You can now confess how much you loved them and the secret things of your heart. Shout it out, or write them a love letter. Get mad at God and tell Him all within you, too. Get it all out. It is all part of the grieving process. The letter will settle in your mind and heart all that is wrong with your uncomfortable, unsettled feelings. You will feel calm after expressing everything within you.

I wrote a letter to Paddy over a year after his death. Here is what I said to him:

*Dear Paddy,*

*Today is a warm sunny day after much snow and gloomy, foggy weather. I hiked down to our favorite rock near the pond, where we lay in the sun and dangled our feet in the water. I rested for quite some time in the sun, basking in its warmth. You would have gotten all wet and sandy by now and then tried to lie on my towel or lap. I would get mad, but not really. It was icky, but I tolerated it. I would love now for you to make me all wet and sandy. I wouldn't mind a bit if you were here with me now.*

*I don't go down to the pond much anymore. Going there makes me think of you and the times we lounged under the clouds or in the sun's warmth. It still makes me cry to be there without you. How could you abandon me and leave me all alone? How could you leave me without your companionship?*

*After I could not stand the loss of you beside me anymore, I climbed Samone's mountain behind our pond. We used to hike there almost every night sitting at the top, looking down at the houses and cabins so tiny below us as the sun went down on our day. Once Marion, our neighbor, took our picture from her back deck laying on our rock, you on my knees like you always did. My hike has been the first time to the top of Samons without you, too.*

*I remember a day when we were at this absolutely amazing pond with a waterfall and a slick rock you could use to slide into the water below. You let me hold you and go down the waterfall. I appreciate you didn't scratch me or cling to me. You went down the fall as if we did these things every day. You were such a sport about everything you might not have enjoyed. I know you did them to please me, just to be with me. I appreciated that about you.*

*As I hiked, I realized I would have to lift you over some rocks you used to jump on. You were getting on in your years, and though you could still hike, you had difficulty jumping. I bought a baby's front pack for you. I was ready to carry you when you could no longer go where we used to roam. Regardless of whether you could not have made it on your own, I would have taken you wherever I went. I would never have left you home alone. We went everywhere together, didn't we? We had some perfect times, didn't we? I am grateful, though you went fast when you did, and you didn't have to struggle to walk and climb rocks. You left this world with your pride and dignity intact, and for that, I am grateful. But I sure miss you, Paddy.*

*Love, from your mama*

I think you will be very surprised how good you feel after writing a letter or several letters, depending on who you may be angry with. You can write one to yourself as well. Write it all in your journal so you can go back later and gather your feelings and watch your transformation. I also wrote to those who were not there for me in my pain. I didn't share it with them, but I felt better and it was easier to forgive them. Anger can cause us to feel ugly or undignified, but anger serves a purpose when we inquire into its depths. Such an emotion causes us to make changes needed for growth and maturity.

Anger may be a very uncomfortable emotion if you are not accustomed to that feeling. If anger is familiar to you, it is time to see what is beyond that emotion. Your progression may be substantial now that you understand anger. You are stronger and more able to adapt and concede your loss. You felt the gamut of emotions and did not die from them. I have given you steps to deal with your anger. Your feelings no longer control you. You control them. Dealing with unforgiveness, which can lie beneath your anger, is as simple as writing a letter. However, if you are living with unforgiveness, you should also look more in-depth with additional books. You will never be the same after loss, but also you will be different because you know how to handle anger and the other emotions involved. Now you will look past the pain to recognize your gifts. Use what you have learned to help others in their grief process. Just don't tell them you understand, though getting darn mad might be just what they need to feel alive again!

*"Anybody can become angry. That is easy; but to be angry with the right person, and to the right degree, and at the right time, and for the right purpose, and in the right way, that is not within everybody's power, that is not easy." ~Aristotle~*

*Sugar–John Mirdo's streak of lightning*

## Points to consider:

- Anger may feel more acceptable than feeling pain.
- This may be an emotion you don't normally express, but these are not normal times.
- You don't need to feel guilt or shame at your anger for the one you have lost.
- Your recovery in this process will be to see what is beneath the anger.
- Unforgiveness may be one feeling beneath the anger. Deal with it too.

## Stage 2 — Anger
## Characteristics:

- Rage
- Hurt, sadness, and loneliness
- Panic, fear, and anxiety
- Resentment
- Guilt,
- Powerless
- Uncomfortable in your feelings and acceptance of those feelings
- Unforgiveness

## Possible action to take:

- You can wear yourself out crying, a good cleansing cry.
- Or go outside, garden, hike, bike, walk, dance, or do anything that externalizes the agony you feel inside. Get yourself exhausted.
- Only be around people you feel fully comfortable with who love you, regardless of your behavior or outbursts.
- Take all the comfort offered to you.
- Forgiveness may be in order to get through the anger, forgiveness of the deceased, and others who say or do the wrong things. Forgive yourself. You are not at fault. Get a good book on forgiveness if this is a problem for you.
- Talk to your loved ones and tell them all you want them to know. Write them a letter or write it in your journal so you can go back later and see your progress.

Question to ask yourself:

- What feelings are beneath all that rage?

You may have been through many uncomfortable feelings of rage or unforgiveness in the last stage. Perhaps you are tired, maybe even exhausted. I have given you many solutions to go through this stage, and you may still have some work to do. Go ahead if you need more work in this area of your life. It will do your character a lot of good. However, the next stage of grief, bargaining, will be a stage of rest and hope. Move forth only when you feel at peace in the last stage.

~~~

*"Our culture thrives on black-and-white narratives, clearly defined emotions, easy endings, and so, this thrust into complexity, exhausts." ~Caroline Knapp~*

# CHAPTER 8
# Working Through the Grief —Bargaining

Bargaining is the stage of grief most associated with hope and rest. The mind is too busy making deals to feel the pain thoroughly. One may be tired from feeling the barrage of emotions in the first two steps, and bargaining may bring some relief, a weigh station of rest.

Though I am describing the third stage of grief, bargaining, you may go back to other steps of grief before moving on. You may also move right on to depression without one thought towards wishing you could make a deal to have a life with your loved one intact. Alternately, you might have begun your grief with bargaining, wondering what you could have done differently. You probably didn't possess all the information to do anything differently, or it wouldn't have made a difference. Whatever you did or didn't do would not have changed the outcome. However, your mind tricks you into thinking there could have been a different result. Your mind wants to occupy itself with "what if" scenarios to avoid pain. It's a way of putting off the suffering, keeping it distant, and finding relief. It is stalling the inevitable, the face of reality. Bargaining never finds a solution.

This is one of those moments where I would love to have made that bargain to have Paddy back.

*I lost Paddy one week ago today. Since I am watching a friend's dog while they are on a ski trip, I became occupied with his care, walking, feeding, and petting, and completely forgot this was the day last week of Paddy's demise. I walked into my house, and it hit me like a dash of cold water in my face. It was that very hour I walked through the door last week—Paddy was wallowing in pain, waiting for me, his mom, to solve what he could not work out for himself. The intensity of the pain returned with the impact of a Mack truck. I could only cry, mourn his death, and curl up in a ball. I was totally and completely demoralized. How can a date trigger pain and anguish when time has spanned the period from the cause of pain to the present? This is my Friday which I am glad about. I do not work tomorrow. I can cry, wake up with puffy eyes and not have to explain.*

*His things are still all about me. Some of the hidden and practical things others can use are going out the door. Some get rid of their pet's belongings right away, immediately throwing their pets' things into the trash, still smelling of them. Others hang onto them forever. Like myself, others keep their belongings as though their pet might return someday and use them again. I still have Paddy's bed by the fireplace, where he used to like to receive* the fire's warmth. If he were not up on the couch near the window where he could spy me arriving home from wherever I had been, he would be curled tightly upon his bed, nestled in his blankie. I found two black and white covers for him. When he curled up in them, one could not tell where Paddy ended, and the blanket began. I still have both blankets, and now and then, I press my face deep within their fibers, glimpsing his scent, reminding me he lived with me and enhanced my life for many years. Paddy brought comfort during my divorce and trials of life. His scent will always be in my heart and mind. I will never forget that scent, or him, ever. Sometimes when I am walking through a room, I catch a faint aura of him lingering in the air as though he had recently passed through the room. I look around. He is not there, but he was.

My friend, Javier, told me recently that he still feels the paw steps of his long-gone pet upon the couch beside him as though he was ready to curl up beside his master. My friend still feels his presence. I believe, as many do, that our pets never truly leave us. They would never consider leaving their owners. They know as we do that with life comes inevitable death. Our pets do their best to let us know they are still with us in spirit. It is up to us to stay connected to that essence. When we hold them in our hearts, we hold on to them in spirit.

I can pretend that Paddy is here since I can still smell him. I can bargain with God. "Lord, if you will let him greet me at the door as he always would, I would do anything, just name it." Even today, I call out, "Hooty hoo" upon entering the house. I still hope he will show his spotted self upon my words of greeting.

I would love to see Paddy come running after a day's work. The cold realization is he is not with me anymore. I can smell him and see what he left behind. Cards arrive in the mail from the hospital and vet, but who will comfort me now? My comfort is gone.

*Upon returning home from work, I discovered a card picked up from the post office that day. It was a sympathy card from Paddy's vet. Obviously, the Emergency Animal Hospital had communicated and made the call. I did not want to tell them not to send any more reminders of Paddy's well-check. He had his exam only one week before his death and received an excellent report of health. He was always in shape, and even after fifteen years of life, that's one hundred and five in human years, he was still active and lively. After all, he was a Jack Russell Terrier. I always joked he was a Jack Russell Terrorist, but he was one of the good Jack Russell. He minded, mostly. He would have been sixteen years old on May 20th.*

*I called Paddy a Jack Russell Terrorist for the terror he caused the coyotes that traversed across our property every day. They would try to lure Paddy into the forest away from the house, other coyotes lurking beyond the trees and upon the road, working together as a pack. I always watched him closely when he was outdoors, just for this reason. One morning, I let Paddy out while it was still dark. The sliding door was open as I went back inside to retrieve my coffee cup. I heard a yipe. I dropped my cup and tore outside. Gladly, the door was still open, or I would have broken through it. There was my little dog on top of the coyote, tearing him apart. I didn't know my loving dog could be so vicious! I didn't think Paddy needed any help and waited to see what would happen next. Pretty soon, the coyote managed to get up and shake himself off. He looked around as if to say, "Gee, I hope my friends didn't see that." Then he trotted off into the trees to the safety of his friends. In a group, Paddy would have been toast, but alone he took care of himself. I prayed he would not follow and grabbed Paddy as soon as I could get close enough, and we went inside to the safety of our home. Paddy just licked himself, and that's when I discovered a puncture wound. I cleaned him up and applied ointment, and he was okay, ready to sit down for our morning coffee and prayers. I am sure that Paddy inflicted far more damage on that unsuspecting coyote.*

Paddy could have readily died that day like any day he fought off a coyote attack. It was not his day to die, for which I am most grateful.

Bargaining is just the bridge between anger and depression moving down the road to acceptance. Bargaining sets us up to see the truth. It suspends us between the more horrible emotions of anger and depression. We still feel like we can control an outcome. Bargaining keeps our sanity for a moment while our brain rationalizes and works towards a solution. Overall, bargaining helps us gain the truth. Once we accept we can't change the outcome, we can quickly speed head-on into depression. These emotions are natural. All these emotions are part of the healing grieving process.

Picking up Paddy's ashes was a blast of reality I was not ready for yet. But each day brings proof that they are not with us anymore.

*My friend, who was with Paddy and me at the hospital, also wanted to be with me, to pick up Paddy's ashes. Today, before work, we headed down the hill to the Gateway Pet Cemetery. We arrived right at their opening hour of eight that morning. A high wrought-iron wall surrounded a grassy area with pet headstones and flowers adorning many of the plaques. The one I could read* inside the fence lived twenty-one years. I bemoaned Paddy's brief life at the sight of someone's good fortune to have their pet for so long. However, I do not lament Paddy's good health his entire life. I never once took him to the vet for anything other than his well-check and vaccination appointments. His ears were flopping around him in exuberance throughout his life until the last hours on earth. We must accept the blessings of having our pets for as long as they blessed us to have them instead of thinking we had been cheated for a longer time. We were given a gift for as long as that may be.

I called the office since the gate was closed. A young woman exited a side door, clutching a little blue bag. I said something about how he fit in one small bag, when before he filled my arms? The girl hugged me. I thanked her and walked away with Paddy in a bag. I took my Paddy bag to the car, where my friend and I tentatively peeked inside. Inside there was a large manila envelope, a small cedar box with Paddy's name inscribed on a gold metal plaque on top, and a small lock and key locking away the very essence of his life. There was also a small mesh bag holding Paddy's paw print. A tear rolled down my cheek. I sat in the car for a minute and lifted the envelope out and gave the bag to my friend. He peeked in the bag and removed Paddy's ashes, quietly digesting the magnitude of his precious life, all fitting into a tiny box weighing very little. He only weighed fourteen pounds at his heaviest, but now his weight was less than a pound. Currently, I plan to make a vignette on a shelf in my house with his ashes, footprint, and picture. Maybe later, I will spread some ashes upon the waters we tread on those hot summer days in our local mountains.

I cried softly on the way home, taking in the poem, along with Paddy's death certificate, and wondering about the ways of life and death. I am not sure, but someone at the pet cemetery probably wrote the poem. It's called:

## Redefined Love

*Do not grieve, for I'm still here.*
*I live in memory and not in fear.*
*I am always with you, night and day,*
*In memories of when we used to play.*
*Your kiss was wetter than my nose,*
*So please dismiss your mournful woes.*
*And reminisce upon my kiss,*
*Of you, this is what I truly wish.*
*Remember all the times we shared,*
*The laughs and moments cannot compare.*
*And know that life is bittersweet,*
*But the love we shared was a special treat.*
*Please dry your tears and lift your head.*
*Because our relationship isn't dead.*
*Our life, a book has not been closed,*
*But a new chapter has been exposed.*
*We will live this new chapter all the way out,*
*Together, with each other, without a doubt.*
*Now take a step forward. I'm right behind.*
*For now, our love has been redefined.*

*The last stanza of the poem is the most telling. Yes, we take that step forward. There is never going back. I must learn to live with Paddy's spirit by my side, no matter that I cannot pick him up and dance and kiss him. He probably never liked to dance anyway, but dance he would, just because it is what I wanted. It never bothered him to do what I wanted, no matter how scary or bizarre.*

Just know that you may forever grieve the loss of a loved one. The pain may diminish over time and not be as acute as the day they died, or bring you tears every time you think about them. However, with the passing of days into months into years, as each year fades behind you, you will be better able to deal with the pain. Today is mom's birthday and for some reason brings pain.

*Mom's birthday*

*I am not at home today, but am acutely aware of the pain of losing Paddy. Some days are more challenging than others. Would it be harder on someone else's birthday, my mom's birthday, or other people's death? Will every death and birth of another trigger the sadness deep within me over Paddy's death? I suppose I will forever be sad over the loss of my greatest friend.*

It may be during these times of triggered sorrow that we can appreciate our loved ones. We can see how others are unique and different from us. Some character traits may have irritated us as when Paddy insisted on going through every speck of crud, I swept into a pile. However, I can laugh about that now. I can more easily see through the annoyances to the charming characteristics he possessed. He had many.

*When Paddy came into my life and my heart, a light turned on. I could see what I had never seen before: a bee on a flower, a speck of something on the floor that was so interesting and worthy of close inspection. I just passed it up like it was a speck of dirt swept up into a pile and thrown away. Nothing special. Everything is new and extraordinary to a dog. Paddy always inspected my dirt pile for some morsel to eat or examine. If we allow ourselves, we can see everything through fresh eyes, everything as unique and worthy of our attention. Each color may become more radiant, each shape sharper, every smell worth picking up on, each sound worth hearing.*

*Pepper—John Mirdo's curious dog*

This next excerpt from my journal demonstrates the ongoing sorrow and the importance of taking the time to grieve and feel your emotions. If we become too distracted, we may never make it through the full process set before us. I may have been suspended between bargaining and depression. It has been hard to tell what stage I was in sometimes. But I know I was always progressing on the road to recovery. Even though you might not know where you are, if you know you are moving ahead, that's what matters.

*April 1st April Fool's Day*

*April Fool's Day or All Fools' Day possesses light-heartedness and foolery. I definitely am not in the mood for light-heartedness. My friends have entertained and occupied me almost continuously since Paddy's death. I know they have good intentions. However, I need the quiet of our home to grieve his loss, with his bed always beside the fireplace where he would warm himself. I still sleep every night wrapped up in his blanket, the merest scent catching my attention, making me look around, thinking he is near. Now that I am in the sanctuary of my home, I allow myself to feel the pain within me, and it expands outward beyond the containment of my heart. Breathing into the pain, I calm my soul. I don't hide it or cover it over with other emotions. I just allow myself to experience the feeling of loss and emptiness. I don't fight the feelings. Grieving allows the feelings to flow and ebb within me and expand and exceed my body's restraint. There comes a release of anxiety and calm acceptance of what is, an acceptance of all I feel. I realize I will go through this process many times before entirely permitting my loss and sensations of sorrow. I must be open to them, not resistant. Expressing sorrow is ok. Avoiding the complicated process of grief and loss will not produce growth and healing. Loss takes time and a great deal of emotional energy. It is tiring and exhausting. I give myself time to rest. I allow time to grieve my loss. It is real.*

In the midst of all your pain is life. The world continues to spin, the clock to tick. Just when you think you can't take any more pain, life may bring more adversity to test and strengthen you. Our problems give us a chance to reflect. We might not understand the dynamics of our lives, but we can find enrichment, relations, and love in all that happens to us. Here is one example of life giving me more than I thought I could handle. There were a few hard-hitting situations I didn't think I could handle when Danny died, too, but somehow I made it through. I progressed mostly through the forgiveness of those who hurt me.

Here is one story of pain I thought I couldn't get through. After all, I had already been through enough in my mind.

*Today ends an incredible three-day holiday in Mammoth with some terrific friends skiing. I am usually the one to care for my friends Bev and Kerry's dog Brody while they are gone, but this time I secured a spot on the trip, and it was up to others to care for and feed Brody. His caregivers were not experiencing a suitable response from Brody about going outside and eating. Finally, today Bev received a text that Brody was not doing well. We skied down that mountain and packed up lickity split, running for home. Everyone had all been hoping Brody was pouting because mom and dad left him, and I wasn't there to spoil him and stay with him. We cried most of the way home. Those last miles home were pure torture. It has only been three weeks since Paddy died, and the pain was raw and near the surface. The tears fell readily, scorching my cheeks. I loved Brody for many years, and the ache was not a trigger this time for Paddy, but for the love of someone else's pet whom I loved as much as my own, and for Bev and Kerry's hurt, Brodie's mom and dad. He was almost fifteen. I knew it would come, but just like Paddy, their demise seems to happen so fast.*

*I stayed with Brody only a couple of weeks ago and we walked every night, and he walked around reasonably. His hind legs were feeble, but he always seemed excited to go out for his walk as he tugged on the leash as soon as I got it around his neck. We arrived back home from our ski vacation and found Brody on the floor by the door with their son Chris petting his head and looking after him. I rested on the floor beside him. Bev was on the other side, wiping his head with a warm cloth, as I wiped the goobers out of his eyes as I always had. I massaged his body, getting all the spots I thought would feel good on a dog who had run miles in his day, hunting with dad, and going on walks. I knew he was dehydrated as handfuls of hair came up on my hand and lined my leggings. When it was time to leave the owners and their dog, I cried all the way home. I didn't want to leave him but knew they needed their time alone with him. I almost can't bear knowing what they must go through, leaving their dog to tromp over the rainbow bridge. Maybe Brody will find Paddy, and they could frolic together, young and vibrant.*

*I woke up crying this morning, just as I had when Paddy passed away. I knew deep in my spirit that Brody had gone home. The text arrived early. He died with his mom and dad by his side at 10:30 that very night. It is another sad day indeed. I will miss Brody enormously, but I am sorry for Bev and Kerry, who I know will grieve their loss. Brody had always been a wonderful dog. He was a pointer from the start, and what could have made his dad prouder? Brody, a hunter, had his day in the sun. He chased a great many ducks and frolicked through flowers. Brody was beautiful in body and spirit, enough to grace the cover of the popular Sportsman magazine. We will all miss Brody. He had taught his owners' many lessons. It was time to go home. Through their grieving, may they learn even more than I have.*

CHAPTER 8

*Kerry and Bev's Golden Retriever–Brody*

As you journey through your recovery, many feelings can unexpectedly arise and cause you to feel uneasy. Some deny their feelings, surmising them to be inappropriate or ugly. You may feel afraid of these emotions. Alternately, you might not know what you feel. Instead, you try to distract yourself through business and caring for others. You have not learned to recognize and feel those emotions yet. In addition, some are not inclined to focus on themselves. It might feel awkward. They never focus inward. They are those who care about others but not themselves. It is also possible that some feelings emerge from the past. One can be confused, not knowing what feelings belong and which don't belong in your current circumstances. These feelings may be unexpressed past feelings that you may not have acknowledged. You must address all these possibilities. One can bury feelings for only so long. They boil over a heated kettle to spill into your relationships and life. Avoiding the complicated process of grief and its associated feeling will not produce growth or healing.

If you feel overwhelmed, you only have to face one emotion at a time. Be gentle and kind to yourself. Give yourself time. There is a season for everything. Everyone who lives long enough will have losses and will need to grieve. Losing someone is not a punishment in life, and one cannot rush these experiences. There is no finish line, only growth. Like the muscles of a runner, we only grow stronger the longer we stay in the race. The finish line means the end of our lives. Don't get in a hurry. Grieving and growing is part of everyone's life if they allow them to be. Grief is a process, not a destination. Face it honestly. Face yourself and your emotions fairly.

Furthermore, you don't have to deal with these turbulent emotions and circumstances by yourself. Grief and pain can take a great deal of emotional energy. However, there can be peace and serenity when you share your pain, anger, and frustrations of dealing with loss in your life. Guaranteed someone out there has had similar feelings over similar losses. Someone to mourn with you helps you bear the grief. When you see how others have traversed the bumpy road of grief, you may detect a hope that you can latch onto for your future. Also, when you share your feelings and feel heard and understood, you may feel a closeness you never experienced with another in your life before this space in time.

Consider that you might be at just the right place at the right time in your life right now, even though you might not like where that is. The refining process is never anything we enjoy until we are through it. Conversely, avoiding the complicated process of grief will not produce growth or healing.

*"Grief is like the ocean; it comes on waves ebbing and flowing. Sometimes the water is calm, and sometimes it is overwhelming. All we can do is learn to swim."* –Vicki Harrison~

## Points to consider:

- Bargaining is a way of putting off reality.
- This stage helps you accept the truth one step at a time.
- Life will go on and you have the chance to slow down and learn about yourself and your relationships.

## Stage 3—Bargaining
## Characteristics:

- You may feel hopeful and a bit more at rest, but only because you are asking "what if" questions and rationalizing.
- Guilt and asking, "What if...?"
- Fantasizing different outcomes
- Rationalization
- Feeling of uneasiness usually near the end of the stage

Possible actions to take:

- Look at those still around to love.
- Do not be resistant to any feelings you are experiencing. Let them flow.
- Try dealing with only one emotion at a time.
- Do not get too busy. You still have a way to go. Rest.
- Share your feelings of pain, anger, and frustration either with a good listener, grief group, or counselor. A counselor at any stage is therapeutic if you need it.
- Write in your journal.

Questions to ask yourself:

- What will you gain by feeling the pain now? What do you have to lose?
- Is there someone who has lost something, too? How can you help them?

The following stage of grief, depression, can be challenging. You have learned many things by now through the other stages of grief. You know to be good to yourself and give the process time, resting frequently. Recognize individual emotions and deal with them one at a time. The most important thing that would be vital to understand is you will not be in this depleting stage forever. You will get through it. If you got through it, you will learn more about yourself. You will be stronger and more able to help others struggling. If you get nothing else from this book, know whatever you go through; there is someone else you care about who will go through loss as well. Then you can be there for them, as others have been for you. Life lessons are about being there for each other.

~~~

*"When you adopt a dog, you have a lot of very good days and one very bad day." ~W. Bruce Cameron~*

# CHAPTER 9

## The Onset of Depression

You will have many good days with a pet or someone you love in your life. However, eventually, someone you love will die. That one very bad day may mean you will eventually feel the weight of depression, not clinical depression, but depression that serves a purpose in the healing process of grief. Clinical depression is persistent, debilitating, overwhelming feelings of sadness and loss of interest in the process and joys of life. This fourth stage of grief is just as overwhelming as clinical depression. It is debilitating with feelings of sadness and loss of interest in life. However, this loss of zest for life is because of your loss. You have a reason for your hopelessness and despair. This depression is something you can overcome. Not everyone will experience this stage, but it can be tough if you do.

At some point, you may feel the heavy, oppressive weight of depression, the fourth stage of grief. This stage takes us from the fantasy of bargaining to the reality that our loved one is truly gone forever. Depression is a deeper level of distress than we have experienced until now. Depression is what it sounds like, a depression of emotions, too horrible to allow expression. As in the other grief stages, one does not get over the emotion—one goes through it.

You may feel depleted and consumed at some point. I felt hollow most days. My tank was empty, and I didn't want to bother to fill it up. My depleted life's blood deflated my spirit. Life took what I didn't choose to give up. I still got up to go to work. I didn't feel like it, but I did. I went to church. I smiled at my friends, but I wanted to curl up in a ball and cry. I hadn't slept, and when I did, I woke up crying. I didn't eat. I wasn't hungry. What would have been the point?

There may be that feeling that an elephant is sitting on your chest. You can't breathe. You don't care if you breathe. It is entirely too much work. You feel you are climbing the highest mountain, swimming in the farthest ocean, and flying through clouds of pudding. The simplest task feels monumental.

You may feel that anguish has ravaged your body like an alien invasion. You sense nothing but pain. Nothing is important but the pain. It's all you feel. Depression is something we don't want to feel, so we shut it out. If you are avoiding involvement with others, your community, and life, you are ignoring the symptoms of an ailing soul. Let yourself feel the pain and cry if the tears are coming, anyway. I stared for hours out the window, all winter, snow falling after Danny died. It didn't matter. Nothing mattered. It was very difficult to connect and fellowship with other souls. It is, however, just what our broken soul needs to heal. Other broken souls will recognize your injured soul and be there for you. Let them minister to you.

You may catch glimpses of times when you think you are going to be okay. Then there are those days when you don't think you can hang on as you slide into depths of sadness. Depression has its way of going so deep that some wonderful memories ease into your mind. This is a good sign and a welcome reprieve from overwhelming emotions. Here are some memories I wrote about in my journal as my soul was healing. Memories are wonderful for the soul. I enjoyed everyone and still enjoy these memories. Write some in your journal too.

*I haven't been home much lately. My friends are making sure of that. But when I am home, I work going through my books. I took down all the books from the shelves, piled them on the floor, and replaced only the ones I would cherish and read, a Marie Kondo method. As I grabbed one off the stack, an old picture of Paddy floated to the floor. He was sitting on our boat's top deck, adorned with a life jacket so young, cute, and innocent. Tears clouded the picture as I remember some of those early days with him. He was not especially fond of swimming in the cold water, but when it was hot, he would let me put him in the water and paddle around until I pulled him out by the handle of his flotation device. He would immediately want in my lap to get his warmth back. I probably hated that as much as he hated the water. One time, I took him down to some ponds in our mountains and held him close while I slid down some rocks into the water. Paddy didn't scratch or claw to get away. He went along with my shenanigans because I wanted to do it. He loved me that much.*

*It has been over a month since Paddy's left my side. I decided it was time to take that first walk alone. My eyes misted over about halfway down the path. I looked behind where my Paddy would be. No one followed. In those last days, he was forever behind me. However, in his youth, my pupster was always in front of me on the trail. I called Paddy when he became out of sight. He would run from up ahead, looking at me as if to say, "I'm up here, making sure it's safe." I consistently wanted to keep Paddy in sight, fearing a wild animal attack. Plus, I wanted to watch Paddy for any reaction to our surroundings. He would shake and shimmy if any wild animal were close. When I looked around, there it was in the distance, a person or wild animal. Paddy was a reliable dog, always aware of his surroundings, and much better at it than me. It was also uncanny that when I called out for Paddy so I could keep him in sight, he knew he only had to show me his face and I would be okay, and off he would run. At other times, when I would call his name, Paddy returned to my side. He seemed to know the difference in my calls.*

*Luckily, two men were approaching from the trail ahead of me. I quickly put the tears in check. After I smiled as though I hadn't a care in the world, I walked on in the forest's silence; the silence shouting at me that Paddy was missing. "Where has your companion gone?" it seemed to say. The quiet accused me of leaving behind my pupster. How could I? What do you inform the accusation of silence? You tell it nothing. You go on and hope next time the silence stays quiet and lets you mourn in peace.*

*Today is Easter and a joyous day indeed. Easter always reminds me of new beginnings. I have the freedom to choose where to go and what I can do. I met up with friends, and the day went well. We're off to church to celebrate. We planned the day, and it*

## CHAPTER 9

*runs smooth as butter on warm toast. After taking pictures of us girls in cute Easter outfits, we are off to the Valle'e d'Brume, a fabulous French bistro. We chose healthy plates of meat and cheese, salads and fruit, and delectable desserts for sharing. We sit outside the French restaurant with our café Americanos feasting on sun and meat and cheese sandwiches. Paddy came up in the conversation. We still look for Paddy because he was always nearby. When I arrived at my friend's house earlier, unloaded my things, and returned to my car to retrieve Paddy, he was not there, and then I remembered. My friend did the same, looking around for him as I unpacked my suitcase. I was not entirely unloaded until Paddy was out of the car. She hesitated to return to the car and then recalled that he was not with us anymore. Even their dog went looking in the car seat for Paddy.*

*I still look for Paddy's face at the window where he would greet me when I drove into the driveway home from work. I always say, "Hooty Hoo," as I walk in the door so he knows I've arrived, and the fun could begin. My home would be empty, and quiet, the air without a whiff of him, my beloved Paddy. I was at my friend's house for the holiday, and I was grateful.*

*Life is not quite as much fun without Paddy. I think when you have kids and pets; it permits you to have fun, be goofy, and all-out foolery. You run, you push, you dodge, and pull on their ears. I did, anyway. I found joy in frolicking on the bed or teasing him under the covers. He would growl when I prodded him, and I would laugh at his expense. If dogs don't laugh, I know they smile, baring their teeth in a comical, non-threatening way. If a dog doesn't laugh, I am sure they experience pure joy in playing, running, finding the wind to stir their fur, and just being with you. Why can't we find fun as easily as our pets?*

I think in this stage of grief when we can bury ourselves in overwhelming sadness, it is good to ruminate on the good times, the times you laughed, and just dwelled in pure love with the pet or the loved one you lost. I faced both sadness and joy on my grief journey–in fact, nearly every emotion known to man.

Here is a dog friend who seems to always be happy and smiling. I hope he cheers you up today.

*Jax–Jonathan McCarty's happiness*

*"The second stage of yearning and searching is marked by a sense of emptiness. The mourner is preoccupied with the person who has been lost, seeking reminders and reliving memories."*
*~By John Bowlby, father of attachment theory~*

## Chapter 9

*Today I am focusing on what is funny. After crying so much yesterday, I just want to laugh. After all, laughter is healthy and pets give us so much to laugh over. I need to take my advice and laugh a bit. I began my day watching funny pet videos and the tears escaping my eyes were from laughing at pet antics. Pets can entertain us for hours with their attention-getting stunts. Mostly they are trying to get our attention. They want us to focus on them, not our phones, computers, or anything else.*

I was never at a loss for laughter with Paddy around. Here we banned him from the kitchen so we could cook. He tried to get us to let him in with his pitifulness.

*Paddy behind a gate*

I recall many times I laughed because of Paddy's capers. When Paddy was a pup, I took him to Petco "where the pets go," to pick out his first toy. He was no bigger than a hamster when we went to choose a toy. I told him he could have any toy he wanted. Paddy *could only reach the bottom shelf but he still chose the most giant plaything on the shelf.*

*His big dog attitude told me right off that he would never back down from something bigger than himself. He reached up and grabbed a huge fluffy ball between his teeth, much bigger than he was. I told him to take it to the check-stand so we could purchase it for him. Paddy ambled down the aisle with his new find. He couldn't possibly see around or over that creamy-colored fluff ball and kept bumping into things. He'd get back on course and walk right in front of people. Everyone jumped out of his way, laughing hysterically as he pranced happily towards the check-out stand. My little pupster was a sight to behold as he took possession of his first toy. It was his and his alone. He finally annihilated that ball, giving him hours of pleasure and hours of laughter for us as he tried to subdue that big fuzzy ball. I sewed it up many times, but eventually, his exuberance took its toll on that defenseless toy.*

Here are a few of the happy memories from my journal that relieved my pain for a spell. Please take the time to re-live some of your happiest moments with those you have loved and lost. They will be your lifeline.

*One year ago, I was in Huntington Harbor, California, on vacation. I encountered many water sports around the harbor. The garage where I lodged held many people toys to experience on the water. I spied the paddleboard and figured it was an excellent place to start. The weather was delightfully warm, so if I fell into the harbor, I would not get chilled. I had never been on a paddleboard and thus neither had Paddy. I put the board in the water and gingerly placed one foot on the board and then the other, balancing precariously. My companion handed Paddy over, and I put him at my wobbly feet. He cautiously walked around the perimeter from tip to*

stern and then placed himself between my feet, deemi
place. We paddled all around the harbor, taking on u
ing on our feet. I considered this great fun, frolic,
exercise. The sun warmed my face, and even though I
keep balanced, I relaxed in a way Paddy could recognize and feel. He took on my relaxed state and enjoyed our activity without stress or anxiety. Pets can detect our emotions and respond to them, giving us what we need for that emotion at that moment. I am sure Paddy felt my peace and countered with ease of his own. We were one at this moment. The experience would not have been the same without Paddy at my feet. He completely trusted me.

We can always trust our pets. We can trust their reactions to events, trust in their loyalty, and eternal love. I know they forever wait for us and are cheered by our arrival. We have faith in them to bring us comfort during the trials of life. They are there for us through all things. We cannot always trust people to do the same. It is not entirely a person's fault that they can't accomplish what pets offer. Our pet's mission is greater somehow than any assignment any human, even Mother Teresa, could achieve as one person. Mother Teresa offered the quote that says it all, "I alone cannot change the world, but I can cast stones across the waters to create many ripples." A pet changes the world, one person at a time, and then that changed person loves others as their pet has loved them.

There have been many days I cried over the loss of my best friend. However, I see many things that Paddy taught me I could use in my human relationships. Much of what I have learned is that love isn't perfect, just as people aren't perfect, but we can love them wholly with unmerited love, a love so pure it resembles the love of a pet.

Paddy was always alert and protective.

*I have trod down the path that would take Paddy and me into our beloved woods with their ponds, streams, and wildlife. I now look around more diligently than when I hiked with Paddy. It is a remote place inhabited by wild animals. I previously watched Paddy for signs of wildlife. He would shimmy and shake if he spied or sensed wild animals or humans. He was perceptive to locate animals a long way off. One time we watched as a family of deer roamed the hillside. Another time, he stayed on my lap while we observed a fox ready to pounce on some unaware ducks in the pond before he spotted us and skittered away. Once close to home, we spotted a mountain lion, and he shook until I thought his fur would fall out. He knew this was a big one, a dangerous one. I picked Paddy up quickly, afraid he would tear after this King of the Mountain. He would be a snack, but I am sure I would have struck that lion with whatever I could find until he dropped my dog from his mouth, smarting from the switch across his nose. Yup, I would put myself in danger for Paddy, just like I would for my child. He was my puppy boy, after all.*

I know Paddy would have done the same for me. When our lives matter less than our loved ones, you know you have the purest kind of love. I was all he had. He needed me just as I needed him. I feel the same about Danny. We both needed each other equally. We always had each other's backs. You may also have lost that person who had your back. You will greatly miss what they brought into your life.

*A neighbor came by today while I worked in my yard. He conveyed how sorry he was concerning my loss of Paddy. He liked that dog, he said, who came to greet him upon the road where he strolled by my house daily, heading down the trail out into*

CHAPTER 9

*the forest. Paddy wasn't as friendly as my neighbor thought. He was protecting our home, his sanctuary, and needed to know who was passing by. It is funny how we humans are associated with our pets. I was to everyone, Paddy's mom, not Diana Lee. Neighbors knew me through my dog because we were always together. I thought I was stronger with time, but I still teared up as we talked about our losses. He had previously lost his beloved cat and felt that compassion towards my loss. He knew my pain.*

No one knows that pain unless they have lost someone or a pet in their lives. Losing a human life is a little different from losing a pet. We have beautiful memories of both. However, with humans, there is pain from an imperfect relationship. Our relationships with our pets are different. They have not hurt us; they never wronged us. Our pets merely love us, wait for our return, and respond happily to see us regardless of how we have treated them. They love us unconditionally, the purest kind of love. Not to say we don't mourn the loss of our human relationships in pain. The connections have just been different. One lesson it takes us humans a lifetime to learn is how to love. Love has its twists and turns, its ups and downs in any relationship as others teach us how to love them, and we do the same in return. However, our pets know how to love us from the day they are born. They don't have to choose to love. Our pets love for the sake of living a life of caring without the complications.

Genuine love respects others' differences. It loves them just as they are, faults and all. Authentic love tries to understand. Love always looks for the best in others. Those who love genuinely do not control or manipulate others to get what they want. They don't hold back or withdraw love for any reason. A genuine lover loves without restriction and loves forever.

It's another trigger day, Mother's Day. It's going to be a tough day. I know you will find triggers regularly and it may sink you into a depressive state. You can use those triggers to remember the good, the memories, and the love.
*Mother's Day*

*It is hard to be a mother when your children have left home, and the only pet you had is now gone too. The empty nest syndrome is no joke. It's real. It is hard. When you are a mom, you feel you were born to be a mom. You love and sacrifice your comfort for the well-being of others. You give all you have. Then who do you give to when they are gone? Moms don't know how to cook for one or two. We can't do small loads of laundry. We need someone to love and look after. Our eternal love needs an outlet. Now, what do we do? I woke up this morning, not knowing what I was supposed to do. I was without my beloved Paddy, and my son had not called to wish me a Happy Mother's Day. Sometimes, when life is not what you expect it to be or things go sadly wrong from the human angle, pet owners depend on their pets to console and comfort them. Now I didn't have Paddy to go hiking deep into the woods, lie around, watch movies, and eat popcorn.*

*Paddy knew what I meant when I said, "let's go watch a movie." He trotted into the bedroom where my big screen resides and waited for me to lift him onto the bed to cozy in for the movie and some buttered popcorn. It would be okay if Zac did not call me on Mother's Day if I had Paddy to ease my pain. I could laugh at my dog, who would sniff each kernel of popcorn and turn his nose up if it wasn't drenched in butter. He would only eat the "good" ones. It would be okay as long as Paddy was near. Today, he was not, and so I fretted, looking endlessly at my phone, hoping my son had phoned, and I just missed his call. It was a lonely day indeed. Zac*

## Chapter 9

*finally phoned, but I had worried the whole day he would not call, and I did not have Paddy by my side to comfort me. It continues to be a lonely life without Paddy, even though I have friends. Your friends are not always available. While your dog is always beside you, close as your shadow.*

*Today I washed Paddy's bed. I had kept it around the fireplace where he would stay warm. Somehow it brought me comfort to see it there every day. One day, it bugged me that the bed remained empty whenever I arrived home from my wanderings. I thought if I just cleaned it, it would come alive somehow with its previous owner. Or I could give it a new life for another dog. When I washed the bed and retrieved it from the dryer, the zipper remained stuck. I could not replace the foam that kept the sides up around the bed to snug in my pet. The cot had become unusable. I kept the pillow that went inside the soft frame, but I tossed the rest of the bed into the trash. Then I cried.*

I see nothing wrong with crying. I have observed many people who think they must stop a tear before, what—it gets out of control? It could, I suppose. We may start sobbing and never stop. Not likely. You will run out of tears, eventually. If we don't bawl all we need to, it will come out later when we least expect it. We might not know why we are crying. Or we may sob over something meaningless. It's, to some extent, like not dealing with our emotions when they appear. We need to deal with them. We need to acknowledge our sorrow, the anguish inside. It is natural, and we need no one's permission to express our pain how we wish. Tears are the natural expression of all our pain. They remind us that our suffering is real—our loss is true.

To me, tears are a sign of courage, not a weakness, as some would see it. When you see someone quickly wipe away a tear, you wonder what else they keep inside. An external show of emotion and tears is a sure sign of life within you. To me, it's a sign you accept all that has come with your loss. Acceptance will also creep in like joy crept up on you. Though acceptance is a step, it will be evident throughout your journey.

*"What soap is to the body, tears are for the soul." ~Yiddish proverb~*

I read in Reader's Digest that tears elicit an endorphin reaction that elevates one's mood. When one is down, this is good news. After a long cry, I feel worn out but always feel better. I wanted to go to work, but I didn't want to cry anymore. I already had my share. However, I would face arriving at work and Brodie not greeting me at my car. Here is my journal entry for that day.

*Today, I went to work, where my doggie friend Brodie would typically greet me. He was not at my car door when I stepped out, and tears welled up in my eyes and spilled out upon my cheeks. Paddy was not there either to greet Brodie. There was double the emptiness. They were friends, now in heaven, romping away in the fresh grass. I put my purse and lunch pail away and went to find Kerry, my friend, and boss at work. He sat on a bench looking out into the forest like he was communing with nature. I hugged him and sat down beside him. He had lost his best friend and looked out towards Brodie's burial spot. He and I both cried.*

*We had both lost our best friends, and we understood how the other hurt. We agreed that no one who has never had a pet will*

## Chapter 9

ever understand how much we could hurt. It's "just a pet," they say, just a pet that understands me better than you ever will, loves me better than you ever will, and will be there more than you ever will. I don't mean to sound harsh, but pets do all these things better than any human, and a non-pet owner will never understand this. Kerry and I talked about missing our pets. We told stories and laughed and cried. We missed them terribly.

I used to take care of Brodie and Paddy, and I would walk down the trail from their house. We went swimming in the pond. When I tried to head back up the path to go to Brodie's home, Paddy would lead him up the trail that headed toward our house. I had to call and scream for them to come back. We were not going home but going to Brodie's house instead. It was hard for Paddy to understand, and Brodie followed him, not wanting to go home yet.

That reminded me of a time I was caring for Brodie, and we walked around his neighborhood. I didn't know the community. Brodie and I walked and walked as I tried to find our way back. I kept asking Brodie to take me home, but he walked on. I was lost. Brody's mom and dad in Canada were unreachable. They could have verbally led me back to their house; however, no one answered. I continued to trudge around the maze of homes up and down hills until their street finally came into sight. Finally, I found my way back. No thanks to Brodie, who would probably have kept going. I was tired that day after our walk. I could laugh now with Kerry over that story. No one had ever taken Brodie for such a long walk, and we were now friends for life.

I also related a story to Kerry about how Paddy used to sit on my lap when driving. I know it's against the law, but though he started in his seat, he somehow wormed his way onto my lap. Paddy never sat in the back seat. That was so beneath him; after all, he couldn't see out the front window. Paddy liked to put his paws up on the steering wheel and look over the dashboard out of the windshield. I would lean over so it appeared like a dog was driving the car to any oncoming traffic. I would laugh every time. It would have been fun to see the other driver's reaction to what appeared to be a dog driving a car. My dog could do anything in his youth, so why not drive a car?

I feel better knowing now that Paddy is youthful and can jump like he used to. He could jump up onto the highest bed, on the couch to look out the window, and onto my chest when I gestured to "come up." I would shout, "bang, bang," and he would drop to his back, feet in the air as if dead. He was a trickster. My pupster knew many superb tricks. He could roll over, dance in a circle, sit pretty, jump up to my chest, hang around my neck, and jump through a hoop of fire. Okay, he didn't jump through the ring on fire, but he was brave enough to do such a fiery trick.

It has been snowing and raining and dreary outside. This weather has been the latest arrival of snow I have seen here in our local mountains. Yesterday I was out in the driveway countless times, loading up on wood for the night and the next morning to have a cozy warm fire against the elements outside. On my last trip out, I spied some bear prints that hadn't been there before. It had only been about an hour since I was out. I was working out and didn't hear as he meandered by my front door. If Paddy was here, he would have alerted me to the bear's presence. He goes crazy barking when there are wild animals present. His bark is different when it's an animal; it's more frantic, almost shrill, piercing the quiet. One evening, Paddy started his hysterical barking near the slider, leading to an outside deck bordering the national forest. I knew that bark. I raced into the living room in time to see a big

## CHAPTER 9

*black bear slam into the sliding glass door. The refraction of the glass moved in, and I thought for a split second the glass would give way. Then, in the next millisecond, the glass moved back into place. Paddy continued to warn me of the bear's presence as I grabbed him up in my arms. I dropped Paddy in the bathroom and shut the door. I grabbed my gun and went back to the glass door. The bear was still waiting for his snack to return, but I wasn't about to let that happen. He never left his spot until I turned off the lights and went to bed. I had to hold Paddy tight, or he would have run upstairs to give that enormous ball of fur a piece of his mind.*

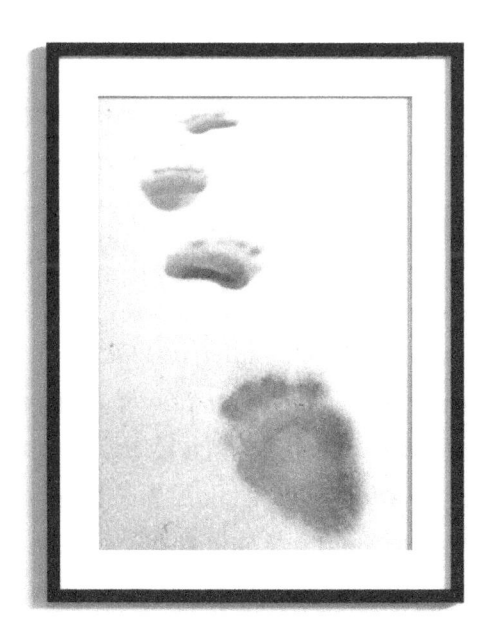

*With the rain and a power outage overtaking my little world, I decided a movie and popcorn would allow me a diversion from the cold house. I don't know if a dreary day was a good day to watch a dog movie, but I went armed with tissues to see "A Dog's Journey" with Dennis Quaid as the dog's owner and his wife, played*

*by Marg Helgenberger. The story begins with a man and his dog. They are as best friends as any pet and human can be, much like Paddy and I, wandering about doing our chores interspersed with some playtime. I grabbed my tissues early in the movie when the man's dog died. The dog was experiencing pain, and not interested in food or play, and the owners called the vet to come and put him down. This scene was about all I could take. I was heaving in my chest, trying not to sob out loud in the movie theater's quiet, but the scene was too much like my experience when I put Paddy to sleep. The vet asked if he was ready to say goodbye, and it was all I could take. The tears overflowed their containment. Just when you think you're getting past the grief's heaviness, it comes bubbling to the surface. It's like no time has passed. It feels like it happened yesterday. Luckily, this man's dog kept coming back as other dogs and living in the man's life by taking care of his granddaughter. Since the dog died at least four times, it kept opening the wound, even though it was not as sad as the first time. I was profusely emotionally bleeding. I lived that moment of death over and over.*

*You might think I'm such a sadist, but those tears needed to fall. Besides, I cheered every time the pet taught its owners something new with each new life. Our pets teach us much about life and how to love and care for others. If we could learn our lessons the first time they teach us, we wouldn't have to lose time before we learned to love when an opportunity is present. We waste so much time mad at someone, prideful, and unforgiving. Ultimately, the four reincarnated dogs offered comfort, protection, companionship, and the dog's ultimate purpose: to love people. Why can't we make that our life's purpose? We strive for so many meaningless things.*

*I have sought comfort in many ways since losing Paddy, but none fulfilling. The pain seems just as acute as the day he died.*

## Chapter 9

*The resolution that he is forever gone is something that I can not seem to find comfort in. I have never felt so alone. I am not lonely. I have good friends for company. It's just that Paddy was my constant comfort. He was always there by my side. Paddy lifted my spirits when no one else could. There is that empty spot beside me where he used to lie, where I could reach out to touch and find comfort continuously. I shall forever miss my pupster.*

*I hiked down to the pond last night and sat upon a rock, watching as the water rushed by on its way to the river at the bottom of the mountain where I live. My tears fell into the stream, disappearing, becoming one with the torrent of water going somewhere I would never go. Only my tears would go there. Luckily, a neighbor and his dog came to comfort me. I came prepared with two of Paddy's chicken chews. I knew sometime I would meet a dog who would take what I offered. She returned a smattering of comfort, a chance to reach out and pet her, soothing my soul for a time.*

*I especially miss my Paddy on a holiday. It's not the typical day when you have your quiet morning routine, run off to work, work all day, and return to be nosed by your dog for a walk. It's the consistency of your daily life that makes the unpredictable more fun and exciting. Paddy always knew something unusual was up on a holiday. He constantly got in my way as I prepared food, blankets, and other fun stuff. There would be gatherings and fireworks. He was unafraid of the sparks and sounds. He just wanted to be with his mamma. I found a bike when we arrived at our location with a basket on the front. I put a blanket in for Paddy, and off we went, wind flying through our hair and ears. Paddy was a flying dog, a fearless super dog hero. He was with his mamma.*

*I know every day I will still be in pain from losing my pet. I attend the Lake Arrowhead concerts in our local mountains, and*

*I see people pamper their pets, giving them their chairs, blankies, and a place in their lives. We humans love our pets. They fill in where life gives us emptiness, where people disappoint us, and when things don't go, how we felt they should. I have met people who have loved the pet of a loved one because that loved one preceded them in death. The pet is all that's left for them. I have seen people love their pets more than their humans. Pets are easy to love. They rarely disappoint.*

*I know pets don't always behave as we expect them to, but we can't expect them to be little furry humans. They are still animals with their own needs and instincts. Some pets are behaviorally challenged due to abuse and over-expectations of previous owners. We can love a pet messed up from treatment before we accepted them into our lives. If your pet misbehaves, it behooves you to give them some latitude, extra love, attention, and appreciation. They give us that much. People deserve as much too, however, they can relate to what tragedy befell them. Our dogs cannot.*

*Unfortunately, pets can't speak for themselves and tell us of the horrific, scary things they may have had to endure. It might not have been the previous owner's fault, only an expectation beyond the pet's scope. Perhaps the previous owner did not understand the dog's breed and temperament and expected more than the breed could produce. Or the pet required more than the owner could give. We never know what our pet has been through if we picked them up after previous ownership. If they could tell us, we could remedy the situation, but they can't. We can only pick up cues and give them what we can. Our ability to understand ourselves and what we offer a pet can also be limited. Perhaps we are not fit for each other. If we genuinely love our pets, we will try to understand the needs that we cannot supply and try to give it or give them to someone who* can. Even giving a pet away can be harmful to them. We must furnish every consideration when having a pet. They are more than we might think and need more than we realize.

It has been a month since my last entry in my journal. I put my grieving aside somewhat for a friend who lost her husband. I can't tell her, "I understand how you feel," because losing a spouse is not like losing a pet. However, I understand some feelings relating to being alone, coming home to an empty house, and nothing being the same because that person or pet is not with you on adventures. I know the emptiness and the pain of loss. I understand the longevity of a relationship you cultivated in understanding the other and making accommodations based on those understandings. We agree it's hard to relate to being uncomfortable around jovial people when you just want to cry. I fathom crying for no apparent reason, just out of the blue of the sky and the green of the grass.

We live expectantly for relief and answers to our painful questions. Our dog, our person, was good. Don't they deserve a healthy life after death? Will we see them in their youth and vigor? Will they be waiting to run across the field of green grass when they glimpse us in our youthful bodies waiting for that kiss and hug? These are questions to ponder and get a clear resolution before the death of a spouse. Don't wonder if they are in a better place and hope for the best. My friend's pain, not knowing if she would see her spouse after her death, was almost more torment than I could take. The uncertainty was her cross to bear. I have peace in believing I will see my beloved Paddy and Danny after my life is over. That peace is a treasure for me to hold on to, whether it is true or not. We all need to believe in something.

If you are feeling depressed, you have arrived in reality. Depression is a state in which your nervous system may shut down, giving room to take in only what you can handle. This step is usually the longest and most difficult. Depression is the stage where you allow the sadness and emptiness to wash over you, like the sea over its beach. Such grounding in your soul may be a place you have never been before. This place may teach you about who you are and what you can accept. The depressive state is where you might sense your aloneness. Most of your friends and family have gotten on with their lives. They expect you to do the same. You are truly alone. Only you can heal your grief. How you feel is normal in consideration of your loss. It is natural to feel such sadness. Again I say, "take your time." This stage is not something you want to hurry, even if it is uncomfortable.

Some signs of depression are hopelessness, overwhelming fatigue, the inability to focus, being unable to sleep or sleep too much, and failing to enjoy the things you commonly loved before. Take an inventory of how you feel. Then accept it as a normal response to your circumstances. Let yourself feel the emotions that arise. Watch movies that elicit both sadness and laughter. Feeling your emotions is key to this stage. You can also recall your favorite stories of the person or pet, write some down, and remember all the joy and love they brought into your life. Appreciate all they taught you.

The key is to recognize the feelings of depression. Once you accept those uncomfortable feelings, you can more easily deal with them. I'm not saying it's easy. None of the grieving process is easy. It is, however, necessary for your recovery, healing, and growth. Get immersed in all the emotions that arise in this stage and add some memories that elicit other more enjoyable emotions at the same time. I have found that one can feel sorrow and joy simultaneously. Watch both sad and funny movies and pet videos and let all emotions merge into one. It will eventually raise you out of your depression. You should not stay in this stage forever. If you feel depressed for too long, see a therapist. Don't stay there.

You can also write in your journal to sort out your emotions. Keep looking back on previous entries. You may discover you made progress and are moving ahead. Seeing progress can lift you out of depression. You can also share your feelings with a close friend or family member. If you talk with someone, make sure you trust them to keep what you say between the two of you. Also, determine if they are good listeners. Some people will listen to you for a minute, then remember a story of their own and talk about themselves. This is about you right now as you spill your guts. Make sure they know you want to talk and them to listen. You extend that courtesy to them someday when they are in need.

Also, keep in mind that your depression may not look like mine. You may experience depression longer or for a shorter time than me, or not at all. As long as you know, you may go through it, and what you can do is what matters. It is a journey as different as mine. You will eventually accept what has happened to your loved one, to you, and to your life. I didn't say you will like it, only that you will accept its reality.

## Points to consider:

- This can be the toughest stage, but the one that produces the most growth.
- Depression can be so deep, it opens your mind to the wonderful memories of that relationship. Don't be afraid to laugh and cry even at the same time.
- Remember, as in any other stage, you will not be here forever.

## Stage 4—Depression

- Overwhelming sorrow and heaviness
- Hopelessness and despair
- Depleted and empty
- Deflated, no energy for living, overwhelming fatigue
- Loss of interest in the process or joys of life, nothing worth doing
- Feeling life ripped you off, and life is not fair
- Inability to focus
- Inability to sleep or sleep too much

## Possible actions to take:

- Allow all the feelings to wash over you.
- Ruminate on the fun times when you laughed and felt the love.
- Appreciate the time you had together.
- Cry if you feel like it and don't feel ashamed.

- Laugh too, at the funny things they did or said, don't feel bad that you laughed.
- Share your stories or write them down.
- Write about all your feelings in a journal.

Questions to ask yourself:

- If it's natural to feel depressed at our loss, why not feel the grief and pain?
- What did you learn about love and life from the one you lost?

Once depression has served its purpose, it will leave just as it came. You will one day catch yourself laughing out loud and realize you just might make it. You will learn to enjoy your life again. When you begin to savor life, you may advance into the acceptance stage of grief. Depression is the very natural phase that prepares one for accepting the loss of a loved one.

*"Sometimes memories sneak out of my eyes and roll down my cheeks." From a book called Annie the truth behind what really happened. ~Mark Myer~*

~~~

*"Love knows not its own depth until the hour of separation."*
–Kabil Gibran~

# Chapter 10
# Moving on With Our Lives —Acceptance

Acceptance does not mean you accept that your loved one is gone as much as you welcome life beyond your loss. "It means you are receiving information about a situation and acknowledging that circumstance as truly happening." It is a neutral intake or observation of what is. Accept means to receive. Acceptance witnesses what is, not the result. It is fluid, a movement. We have more power than we realize following acceptance. Acceptance is not the only action available to us. We can get stuck in suffering or resistance. Or "we can let go of resistance and experience the emotions and reality." (Maddisen K, Krown, contributor of Huffpost blog Sept. 9, 2010, updated, 11-17-2011) We will learn later in the chapter how to nonjudgmentally accept the reality of our situation. You will do this for the rest of your life.

Acceptance differs from "moving on with your life." People will say it's time to move on. It is time to accept the fate and reality of your loss, and your life circumstances. Nothing is truly the same after a loss. You will never be what's called *moving on with your life*. Moving on denotes continuing from wherever you left off. This is not the case when you lost a loved one, be it a pet or humankind. It will forever change your life.

As you go through the grief stages, you will eventually start feeling alive again. There may be no smooth transition from one step to the next. You may be in more than one stage and feel very confused. If you feel confused, frustrated, or resistant, it is because you don't want to accept your reality. Those feelings are natural. "The negative emotions are telling you something is out of alignment." (Maddisen K, Krown) Positive emotions are easier to accept but may be a rare occurrence in the process until later. You may have experienced some already. You will experience more as time passes. Be aware, acceptance is not rebirth after experiencing the other stages. It can emerge about anywhere in the recovery process and continue to grow as you advance through adversity.

Acceptance is admitting you are grieving and you are not in control of your losses.

Acceptance may also mean that you can accept a peaceful day, a joyful moment, and love expressed even while experiencing the pain of loss.

Acceptance can also mean focusing on yourself for a time and administering self-care. You may have felt physically, emotionally, mentally, and spiritually exhausted and confused. Acceptance is knowing you have been through the wringer. It's accepting the time to heal. If you remember what I said about mourning being a self-centered process, know that self-pity and self-care are two different things. Self-pity keeps you stuck, self-centered, and powerless. Self-care is knowing you aren't good to anyone until you care for yourself. The process of grief is difficult and takes time. It needs ongoing attention. When conflicts don't get resolved, our character and soul need care and attention. It is during care for ourselves that we grow and mature. When we learn to accept our loss and all it encompasses, it is easier to move ahead to enjoy life once again.

Growth and maturity indicate acceptance is not outside ourselves but begins with us. One can find relief and a healthy sense of self and empowerment in acceptance. You are not disrespecting your lost loved one but respecting your right to live on without them. I found I did not want to give up my sorrow because I was afraid I was accepting my losses and wasn't ready. I attached myself to the pain in respect for the lives I shared with both Paddy and Danny. My suffering was not so much from the pain as my inability to release the emotion. You are not letting go of the person when you let go of the painful emotions. One can let go of one without the other. I needed to let go of the resistance to the emotions surrounding letting go, accepting my loss.
The next paragraph will give you guidance.

I learned from both Maddisen Krown and Tara Brach from *verywellmind.com* the method of radical acceptance. Acceptance is a slippery concept. However, I have tried this method that works for acceptance of all things. The two women have basically the same technique of acceptance I give you. This works. Tara wrote a book called *Radical Acceptance: Gateway to Love, Wisdom, and Peace*. I also watched a video by her that leads you through the steps of acceptance. These are resources you can call upon when you are ready.

Tara tells us radical acceptance is untraining ourselves from our survival conditioning. Most of us tend toward reaction versus intentional responses. It protects us. When we feel assaulted with loss, criticism, or judgment, we want to protect ourselves from hurt. We quickly respond to the perceived offense to save ourselves, our pets, or our family. This defense is useful in instances such as physical harm. However, most of the time, our reactivity is a defense against emotional pain. The trick to preventing quick responses and resistance is to let those feelings be. Like the cat in the wet paper bag I showed in a previous chapter, let go of what you are feeling and allow yourself to react in wisdom and love. Acceptance is not a passive endeavor, but an active response to your situation based on intellect instead of survival conditioning. The more we interrupt old patterns, the more capacity to enlarge our possibilities. This complete process of acceptance is the pathway to peace and wholeness.

Dorthy Hunt says, "A heart space where everything this is, is welcome." That is the essence of experiencing the steps. It is a mindful presence that is not at war with your feelings.

## Chapter 10

## Steps to Acceptance

1. The first step is experiencing or witnessing an event. You will want to react. It is not time to respond. You are learning not to react or respond yet. You are learning to respond wisely with wisdom and love.
2. The second step is accepting what is truly happening. You only need to know what you are feeling. Use the emotions chart if you need to. You worked on that in the chapter on stages of grief, where you learned how to detect and identify your emotions.

Give attention inward. You are asking yourself, "What is happening inside me now?" Pause and say to yourself, "I see your fear. I see you sadness, anger, frustration", whatever it is you are feeling. Acknowledge the feeling and invite it, "to have tea," as Tara says. Then pause, letting it be. I'm not saying this is any easier than recognizing emotions. Remember, grief has slowed your pace for a reason. Its purpose is to work through this tough stuff. This process is something you cultivate just as you learned to identify emotions and care for yourself. Learn and practice.

3. The third step is responding to the event: good, bad, or neutral. This is an inner choice, not an outer activity. Tara asks, "Can I deal with this or let it be?" This step is recognizing how you feel about all you feel. There is a loop of obsessive thinking that I can get caught up in. I resist, "letting the thoughts be." I judge, I pile on more evidence of wrongs in the

situation, and try to control my feelings. This kind of thinking usually makes me madder or sadder. This procedure keeps me locked in the loop of the same thoughts. I haven't arrived at a solution. It is how we judge ourselves concerning our feelings that keep us trapped in the never-ending loop of obsessive thoughts. When we let feelings be, other things rise in us, such as wisdom, compassion, and care for others. These emotions rise from between the cracks of judgment if we allow them. It is only then we are ready to respond positively.

4. Now is the time for action. We have done enough, having our feelings for tea. We have either let those feelings be without judgment or dealt with them. Letting them be or dealing with the emotions has allowed healthy emotions to rise. Compassion, love, and wisdom have seeped through our judgments. Action is now based on conscious thought rather than on our reactive conditioning to protect ourselves. It is through conscious thought and clarity that we can give ourselves the freedom to accept that there is nothing wrong with our feelings.

The action process empowers you to release the negative emotions or the ones not useful to you.

Eventually, you must begin making choices. There was a time back in the grief continuum that says if you don't start making choices, you may die, too. You may have wanted to die back when you lost your pet or loved one. However, you most likely have glimpsed times recently in which it felt good to laugh. You felt something besides the emotions of grief—some love, a sense of accomplishment, some humor, some joy, or even elation. It's a relief to join in. You have much to choose from, though you cannot choose from what was not offered, that life back. There is life in your choices, fun, and mystery. Sure, you miss your loved one. Be aware those still living could go at any time, too. A new day is promised to no one. You miss the memory of that person, some things you went through together and don't want to forget. However, now is the time to make fresh memories with those living. It might be time to play.

*Buckshot loves the snow*
*So new to him!*

*Summer and Max enjoying the lake*

*Did someone mention play? I love to play with my friends. Paddy taught me to stop and play at a moment's notice. Paddy taught me that playing does a body and spirit right. Today, my friends and I will enjoy each other's company at a winery with its fresh smell of turned soil and growing grapes. We are all long-time friends, close, with no friction, no fuss, much like my dog's relationship. The companionship is soothing and as comforting as my dog's company. Friends are so important in our lives. I don't know what I would do without my friend's encouragement, accountability, and humor. When the going is tough in life, we rely on friends to help us through. We can count on them to help us see our follies and find humor in our mistakes. Friends remind us they care for and love us. Friends do what we can do for ourselves. Even though we can do these things for ourselves, they want to make us feel special enough to go the extra mile. Let them. It is their way of comforting. When one has friendships like these, one*

## Chapter 10

*knows life is good. Even though I no longer have my companions, Paddy or Danny, I can still enjoy lifetime relationships and forge new ones. Friends are not always as readily available as dogs. But with planning, we can get together and forget about life's worries for a time and play.*

As we explore options, we realize we have alternatives and choices. We can choose to stay home and mope in sadness or get out and stir up some fun, even if it feels incongruent with our feelings. It is time to make some decisions. The decision to get on with daily habits before the loss is a good start. I feel more like myself when I get up and get cute, even if I'm not going anywhere. When I indulge in rituals, I feel more accepting of my situation. I struggle less inside myself. Letting go of the struggle creates calmness and acceptance. Make one promise to yourself today to add back a habit or give yourself a new habit to begin. As I was accepting the challenges of my situation, I realized it was time to take on a challenge I could control. I accepted a challenge from a man I listen to every morning.

*Darren Hardy challenges the listeners to his program, "Darren Daily," to be the exception, and go the extra mile. He teaches us to become more, be the best we can be, and live a life of excellence. He recently challenged his listeners to make changes in our lives, affording us time, strength, and commitment to run, walk, or hike for a mile every day all summer long. Darren has dared me to push myself. He challenges his followers to run at least a mile consistently for ninety days. Darre heard of a man people call Raven, who challenged his adversity by running to ease his frustrations and disappointment in life. Raven is the star in the book,* Running with Raven: The Amazing Story of One Man, His Passion, and the Com-

*munity He Inspired, authored by Laura Lee Huttenbach. (2017) Raven (Robert Kraft) has run Miami beach's eight miles for forty years no matter what, no matter what the weather, no matter the injuries. Raven inspired Darren Hardy with his story, who encouraged his followers to imitate the man who challenged himself during hard times. It has been this challenge to himself that kept him running, not from his problems, but running headlong into them. I say this to explain that the challenge is tough because Paddy, my companion, won't be joining the challenge. There is emptiness by my side while I take that early morning hike by myself. He cannot take part in the challenge. I must go alone. I run like I'm running from my grief. In reality, I know the suffering and emotions I am experiencing are part of healing. No matter if I kept running, the feelings would catch up with me, eventually. Feelings travel faster than we ever could. Reading Raven's story could inspire you to challenge yourself.*

It feels good when you arrive at acceptance and realize you have choices. You can open yourself to small or large tests depending on your temperament. I always go for enormous challenges. This challenge gets me back out on the trail where Paddy and I spent many days traversing the mountains behind our home. It also prepares me for an even more difficult trial, The Tough Mudder. My son and I decide to prepare our bodies for walking and running some miles plus overcoming a course of obstacles, much like the military uses to train recruits. This challenge has two purposes for me. One to get out there without my companion again. The other is to prepare for the Tough Mudder. It is harder to start something hard than it is to continue with it. Here are some of my thoughts after starting and some things my pet taught me about being consistent.

## Chapter 10

*I have been going up some steep trails, improving on my Raven Run Challenge. I'm challenged to run consistently, persistently every day for ninety days, no matter what. Paddy taught me that consistency is good for the body and soul. Though Paddy, my beloved pet, is longer alive to engage in my newest challenge, I go, nonetheless. I have taken up the gauntlet. When you don't feel like it, do it anyway.*

*I like to sit down for just a second or two in my comfy antique rocking chair, looking out my big picture window at the National Forest every day after arriving home from work, when Paddy was alive. I would remove my shoes and sit back. He would politely sit in front of me and stare as if to say, "When are you putting on those shoes you wear to walk me? I will wait." Then patience leaves his little body, and impatience takes over. Typically, Paddy was patient with all my shenanigans, but not when it comes time to go outside for our walk. The longer I sat, the sooner he would whine. One should never delay when it's time to play. Play is highly critical to a dog, and it should be to us humans as well. We work, get busy, and keep going. If we don't give ourselves recreation, we will fry ourselves out and drown ourselves in anxiety. Play helps us deal with the overwhelming chores and responsibilities in our lives. Entertainment rids us of the load of stress we take on our shoulders. Frolicking is exhausting, which drains the worries and anxieties right out the front door. Play is refreshing. Play is necessary for good emotional and physical health.*

I am not saying you will feel good every day when you play. Some days will still be hard and may be hard for a long time. Acceptance is part of realizing there will be good days and bad days.

*I felt overwhelmed with a heaviness in my heart as I did my Raven Run. Every day, I run into the feisty little dog who runs with his mom or dad daily as they exercise. I always bring that little dog a cookie or two from Paddy's stash. As the dog ran away with the last cookie in my pocket, I cried. I believed the pain of losing Paddy was subsiding as I accepted he was gone, never to return. I think the weight that overcomes our hearts is the pressure that causes tears to overflow, releasing some burdens of pain and grief. As I looked upon the ground, tears clouding my eyes, I looked to see small wild rose petals where people and animals had brushed against the bush, causing them to fall to the ground. It was a reminder that things like rose petals and tears must fall. Perhaps those things falling to the ground nourish it and make other things grow. It is the natural cycle of the earth and things.*

## Chapter 10

*God says He keeps all our tears in a bottle. He will have enough of my tears to flood the earth, just like in Noah's days. Some days I cry a river of tears. On other days, all I feel is sorrow. How can someone overcome the grief of sixteen years with a beloved pet? One day at a time. One moment at a time.*

With each passing day, we have the choice to dwell on sadness and loss or reverse direction and immerse ourselves in gratitude. Our mind can be a pit to fall deeply into or as open as the sky. Look up into the sky and find gratitude instead.

Each day is a gift, and I thank God daily for all He has given me and everything He takes away. I write in my journal to help remind me everything He does is for my betterment. It is hard to see God's goodness when we lose something or someone precious to us. It is hard to appreciate what He removes from our life. Our journey is not the same, and it scares us. We feel off course. Finding a new way is hard. We search for peace. Here is my entry after enduring much sorrow over the loss of Paddy.

The following excerpt is from my gratitude journal:

*"I am seeing death as a miracle as much as birth. Both are miraculous forms of the cycle of life God created. I feel honored to have been at Paddy's side when he crossed over into God's world of freedom, youth, health, and eternity. When I arrive, I can join him to romp and play, yes, play and play to our heart's content, never worrying about chores to complete or a place to be. I am grateful for God's boundless, endless love. He chose me, just as Paddy chose me. It is a love that overflows, guides, teaches, comforts, and exhibits compassion. His love never ebbs and tides but flows continuously as a river to the sea. It flows into me, then out*

*of me into others so that they might see God. Thank you, Lord, for being with me each day as I grieve for my Paddy. You guide me every step into the long walk into forever. I know you love me unconditionally, just like Paddy loved me. You created our pets who love us, as you do, to demonstrate your love here on earth. Love is wondrous, indeed. Who can understand its depth? It is a gift every day to open—it surprises, delights, and brings joy."*

Losing our pets or someone we loved feels like a loss. However, there is much left behind we were too blind to see while they were with us. Now we are free to see what they taught us, and what they gave us. They come to fill the loneliness and emptiness. In everything, there is a season. The sun follows the darkness of night, spring with its growth, and flowers follow the chill and bleakness of winter. We are bound by winter's wind and cold, to run into the freshness of the budding of spring, breathing in the green smells of fresh growth, the aroma of the sun's warmth like cookies fresh from the oven. Following our losses are new people, new experiences, new love, and new beginnings. The love we learned to cultivate in our relationships with the one we lost, we give to others. One can never waste love. Once given away, it flows like a river to the sea, washing over beaches far away.

I still shed tears over life without my beloved Paddy. We were so much together, so much more than either of us alone. As with all relationships we both gave, we both received. We changed into another entity different from the parts. Humans need to be friends, partners, lovers, spouses, family, neighbors, coworkers, and all the other relationships in between. As iron sharpens iron, we refine and perfect each other's growth and journey. We share what the other does not know. We see another's perspective. Solutions are born from any relationship. We toss together love and companion-

*ship, and they become like tossed salad. The salad is crunchy, soft, bitter, spicy, and maybe sweet through the different ingredients. Each element of a relationship adds a dimension to our lives that forever enriches and expands. We can't remain the same once we have the comfort of loved ones, ideas through co-workers, perspectives of elders or youth, or the mirror of who we are through those closest to us. I still cry for all the wonders of the world that Paddy has taught me and for losing the things I might learn from him if he were alive now. I just miss him so much.*

When you miss your loved one so much, you might fall into depression again, unless you remember what they taught you about life and love. Edge yourself instead into the enrichment and deep fulfillment of life. It does us no good to live every day in the cycle of confused, hopeless, or emotional thought patterns that can damage the soul. We should be slowly moving into experiences of conversing, responding, and self-respecting actions of self-care. In the beginning, it was good to recognize your feelings, but one cannot dwell there.

Here I try to move forward in fun with my good friend. There was some joy and some sorrow.

*I had a perfectly wonderful weekend with my good friend Laura in Los Angeles. We gallivanted around the town, taking the metro line to our destinations. We attended the USC/UCLA football game and cheered and relished all the activities, people, and smells of food cooking. I felt like I was living; all my senses were alive and active. As you entered the coliseum, the smell of the rose garden was soft and sweet, wafting and mixing in the air with the spicy scent of sausages, onion, and peppers of the vendors selling lunches. We walked about, taking in every sight, sound, and smell.*

*I felt more alive than I have in months. The last night in our hotel overlooking the city's lights was restful and peaceful, each room quiet and snug.*

*The following day was active as we packed and prepared to leave for our home in the mountains. Laura wanted to stop and do a few errands on the way home. Our first stop was PetSmart. Pets are welcome in the store. The store was where we would take Paddy for additions to his never-ending pile of treasures and treats. He always remembered where they kept the bins of animal snacks. I was looking forward to seeing some pets there at the store. As I have already indicated, I will love every pet that walks by me or attempts to walk by me. Very few animals escape my caressing and loving when they cross my realm. I just must lavish them in love. I carry doggy cookies in my pocket for those less than enthusiastic about my crossing into their territory. Some of the regular doggies come to expect that morsel. Laura went to choose some new toys for her dog left at home while we entertained ourselves in Los Angeles. There were rows of toys and goodies for pets. As I looked at little seasonal sweaters and toys, I became nostalgic over the many coats and outfits I had purchased for Paddy.*

*We had our matching raincoats and sheepskin coats for the rainy and coldest days in our mountains. I immediately became sad at the thought of my beloved Paddy now gone from my life, never to wear those sweaters and coats I kept. Tears started streaming down my face, and embarrassment overwhelmed me. I tried looking at the fish tanks, my face close to the glass to hide the tears from curious shoppers. Soon my eyes were so clouded I couldn't see the floating pets. I found my way out the door and let the tears flow. Yup, I still sorely missed that little guy of mine, and though the pet store seemed like a good plan, it did not seem like a good idea after looking around. Nine months later, I still pined for my Paddy. I suppose I always will, but I hope someday I can go into PetSmart and pick out a new dog and take him home to pay attention to all he has to teach me about life, love, and yes, even death.*

There will always be those triggers that will elicit sadness or regret over your loss. There will also be "firsts" the first time you do something without your loved one. It will hurt and that's okay. It is natural and normal.

*Paddy sniffing out his Christmas goodies*

Christmas day:

*It was hard today, as any holiday is, to be without my Paddy. He was so much a part of everything I did. Paddy loved Christmas as much as we did. He knew ahead of time what stocking was his and tried to open it early one year by snatching a chew stick from the stocking's top. When I caught him, he jumped down from the fireplace and looked at me with innocent eyes as if to say, "What* are you talking about? I was just getting warm by the fire." Last year I invited guests for Christmas, his friend Petey and my friend Jan. I filled stockings for both Paddy and Petey. Paddy had always been such a piggy with treats and toys—however, this year, Paddy was gracious and did not steal Petey's treasures. Somewhere he had learned to share.

As I recall, when Paddy was young, we took him everywhere. When we visited someone who had pets, we would bring each one a doggy bone. Paddy would play that "come and chase me" game with each dog, and when they left their treasure unattended, he would circle back around and steal and hide it. Then he would go through this chase game with each dog present until he possessed every delicacy! That smart dog would pile the treats between his paws possessively and growl at any dog that came within sniffing distance. He was such a piggy.

I want you to always remember the funny stories and wonderful memories as you go through your healing process. It will bring your loved one alive and you will come to appreciate all they were to you. It is the fun memories that will heal you.

It is a chilly day in our mountains, and it reminds me of a day far and away when I had another neighbor whom I loved. She was an older gal living with her dachshund across the street from us. We enjoyed many conversations over coffee and her wonderful warm grandma cookies. Paddy did not have many friends, but my friend, Darlene's dog, was one. They would frolic as we chatted and never quarreled over anything. Their temperaments matched each other.

Paddy mostly stayed within the property's parameters even though we didn't have a fence. He seemed to know the boundaries.

# Chapter 10

*However, since he had a friend or two around the neighborhood, he would sometimes disappear, and I would receive a text or picture of Paddy visiting his friend. One such time, my friend sent a picture of Paddy high on a stack of pillows watching TV. Oh, brother!*

*I have neighbors, Don and Marion, who watched Paddy sometimes when I went home to Alaska. They walked Paddy and spoiled him while I was away. He trotted down to their house occasionally to say, "Hi" in his doggy way. They would pet him, give him a treat, and send him home. He obeyed and came back home the way he had left.*

*Another time when Paddy did not come back soon enough, and no texts or pictures featuring my pet materialized, I became worried. We live in the national forest with wild animals roaming about any time of the day or night. So, I began to search and call for Paddy. As I rounded the corner, calling for Paddy, he came trotting arrogantly down the road. I looked at him, trying to make out what was on his back. As I got closer, I discovered him wearing a little plaid coat with a turned-up collar around his neck. Someone had given him a coat to keep him warm. He thought he was so stylish and cool! His attitude was one of "certainly I can't be in trouble for being gone so long. I am just too cool." Oh, brother again! My friend and neighbor had donned him in the coat shortly after his visit and sent him home.*

*I haven't written in my journal for quite some time. However, there is not a day that I did not think of my pupster, Paddy. Every day I miss him, with every breath I take. I missed him for Valentine's day because he was my love and the love of a pet is not the humankind. His love was unconditional and pure. I was his universe. Nothing in his world was as important as I was. He waited each day for my waking movement about the house sig-*

naling good things for him. Then later, my arrival from work for our much-awaited walk and a rousing good time in the woods and rocks, all about our home.

I miss him every morning during my quiet time. He would sit beside me in the morning while I read my Bible and prayed. He was quite unlike people who feel they must talk or watch the weather on TV or somehow disrupt my quiet time. I appreciate he didn't make me take him for a walk or feed him right away in the morning but waited for me to let him out and feed him. He didn't overpower me with his needs while I sat in peace, talking to God. He just cuddled and gave me warmth, the warmth of his heart, and warmth on my feet.

The anniversary of Paddy's death is fast approaching, and I dread it will be an entire year in which he left my life. I still see in my mind's eye the last time I saw him lying on that table and regret that I did not pick him up and hold him in his last breath. I thought he was in too much pain and fragile, but perhaps the pain medication they gave him was enough for me to hold him. We should not live with regret. I long to embrace him now and dance about our living room in my exuberance. I shared my every joy and sorrow with him, and he was such a good listener, looking at me with those thoughtful, dark brown eyes. It was as if to say every perfect thing he would tell me if he could. I felt every perfect word he would say. He would say, "Hey, it's ok, I feel your love. I know you have always loved me and did the best you knew how to care for me and give me the life any doggy would want. I know you put me before your own needs sometimes. Even in your discipline, you knew you were making me a better dog to take with you everywhere. I would behave, and discipline would help me act appropriately. I knew you were always trying to keep me safe even

## Chapter 10

as I frolicked in the woods on our walks and in the early morning when the coyotes were out waiting to snatch me. But mom, I got them on the run. There was no need to worry. I looked out for you, too. We were good together, weren't we, mom?" Yes, we were good together. We needed each other for a time such as this. We gave each other what the other needed without words. I could use you today, Paddy, but I know you are frolicking in another world, and we will see each other again someday, and I will have to be content for now. I love you, Paddy. I always will. I accept you are no longer in my life, but I don't have to like it.

Today I received my pet magazine reminding me of Paddy's well-check appointment. As I picked it out of my mail, tears fell. It was time for Paddy's well-check, but also the anniversary of his death. I let the tears fall, and pain fills my heart. My life and home still feel as empty as the night I came home from putting him out of his misery forever. I suppose it doesn't feel as acute, but discomfort rises to the surface from where it is hiding as I go about my business, rising to meet me in a hallowed place.

I long to be tripping over him at every turn. He will clean up after me, so I want to leave the small morsels on the floor. I long to pull on his ears in puppy play and irk the heck out of him like he annoyed many others with his games. I long to hurry home to break him from his long spell of sleep and see if he found all the treasures I left him for his long day at home.

The day of Paddy's passing is only days away, and I contemplate what to do for the day. I want to hang on to his little wooden box of ashes, feeling the weight of it feels like he is still around, even if it's just on a shelf. I don't feel like I could sprinkle his ashes over the pond where we spent hours laying on the warm rocks in the sun, watching as ducks landed on the water and clouds *covered the scorching sun for a moment of relief. It's raining this week, and it's forecasted to continue. I couldn't lie around looking out the window at the rain without him looking out too, deciding whether we wanted to don our matching blue raincoats and walk, anyway. The showers will be dull and gray and match my mood. However, if I walked in the rain, you couldn't tell I was crying... still after a year of missing him.*

March 17th St Paddy's Day

Today, a year ago, I told my friend how Paddy received his name. All the holidays have been hard without Paddy, and I will think of my loss every holiday for years to come, I'm sure. St. Paddy's Day was his namesake day. Currently, we are under lockdown because of the Coronavirus. A friend exposed me to the virus, and as a caregiver, I can't subject her to it. Even though I am not sick, I'm tainted. I am at home for two weeks before I can be in others' presence. I am content to be home, but wishing Paddy could be here with me. He would think we were on vacation, home every day, the fire going, and delightful smells coming from that room where morsels fall to the floor so readily. We would snuggle under the covers while I read a book and laughed or cried out loud, and Paddy would know everything was okay. However, this is the new life I must accept.

It is almost impossible to live a life without loss and pain. However, you have learned how to handle it. You are more able to see what is coming more clearly. Learn to make small decisions and take part in life again. You may decide to play and apply self-care and gratitude. It is time to accept every part of your mental, physical, and emotional self. You may also experience unforgiveness in your life. That journey can be ongoing. However, peace is not as elusive as it once was. A calm acceptance and contentment may be on the horizon. Watch and see.

While you are learning to accept your loss, you may feel uneasy at times. You will also feel other emotions besides pain, some that hurt and some more favorable. Don't compare your grieving with others. Just experience the spectrum of emotions in your way. You will see what life has left behind and what you can choose from in the acceptance stage. We have options and the living are still around us. Life is short, no matter how long it is, and we better learn our lessons while we can.

Acceptance may mean getting through the day or just the moment. Tomorrow will have enough worries of its own. Take it one day at a time. Make one decision at a time. Take on a challenge, no matter how small. The steps to acceptance are very much like the steps of experiencing your emotions. If you cultivate these techniques, you can use them to accept anything in your life. Acceptance happens a little at a time, not all at once. Then one day, you will know you have accepted what happened, and your loved one is gone forever. Moving on will mean taking who you have become and living a new life without your loved one. It will also mean recognizing who is still in your life to love.

In the acceptance part of our grieving, we realize we do not have the power to change our circumstances. However, we can change how to respond to loss. We change only what we can and accept what we can't change. I learned a prayer one time that comes to mind every time I think I am in control, but realize and accept that I am not. Many of you may recognize the:

**"Serenity Prayer"**

*God grant me the serenity
To accept the things I cannot change
Courage to change the things I can
And the wisdom to know the difference.*

# Points to consider:

- Acceptance is not a final destination as much as a fluid movement towards it.
- Growth and maturity grow alongside acceptance.
- You will be "accepting" for the rest of your life.

# Stage 5 — Acceptance

- You may feel more often feelings other than grief.
- You may catch yourself laughing and feeling joy or elation.
- You may see more clearly and look to your future.
- You can now start to make decisions. Don't tackle any life-altering ones just yet, unless you are forced to, to be financially secure or safe.
- You may still feel uneasiness. Acceptance does not mean you are at total peace over your loss.
- Acceptance reminds you, you are not in control of anything but your own responses.
- You may have a peaceful day, a joyful moment, and feel loved and loving.

## Possible actions to take:

- Do not compare your grief with anyone else's.
- Have something to believe in.
- Take time for self-care, whatever it is, to pamper yourself.
- Join in where you feel comfortable.
- Play.
- Get into some good habits and challenge yourself at something.
- Realize all you have to be grateful for.
- You might also find it helpful to continue with any forgiveness needed.

## Questions to ask yourself:

- What have you learned about yourself?
- Who are you now having learned from and loved this person or pet?

There is more beyond the professional's acceptance stage. I added "finding meaning in life" because there was more work to do after accepting your loss. I talked about finding meaning in one's life back at the beginning of the book because when one has gone through grief, it can be an empty life without living in usefulness. We live and learn through our pain. What we learn seeps deep into our souls. It is that changed soul that can help others through their trials. Vitality rises from a healed soul. You can more easily love and allow love into your life. Use your vitality, peace, and wisdom to help others. Doing for others has far more healing benefits than one might imagine. Heartbreak can change us for the better if we so choose. We can move into a serene and joyful life that we can share with the world around us.

~~~

*Sarah*

"Heartbreak is life educating us." –George Bernard Shaw~

# CHAPTER 11
# Finding Meaning in Life Again

Finding meaning in life is a stage I added as I realized there was more work after acceptance. Life has a purpose beyond your comfort, pleasure, or acceptance. You need a reason to rise every morning, go on, and finish strong. Those who have meaning in their lives enjoy greater well-being. They are happier with a purpose in everything they do or say. Open your heart and spiritual eyes to see what you missed before. The process of grieving and understanding how to live through it results in wisdom, growth, and maturity. Loss integrates into your life, teaching you how life, love, and death change you into whatever you want to be. Everything happens for a reason. You won't know the reason readily, for a long time, or maybe never. Understanding the dynamics of your circumstances is not as important as enhancing your character. Integrating your experiences transforms you over time. Allow good to rise from your adversity. Let all things percolate to form values, beliefs, and a character you'd be proud of. If you are still alive, you have a purpose in your living. Your life matters. Make it count.

Innocence lost during the process is inevitable. You will never be the same person you were with this person or pet in your life. You grow into someone new. It's possible to find meaning in your skin. You know who you are, and your desires for the rest of your life. Everything you do will be different. You will see how you can be useful, living out your purpose. You find peace amidst the sorrow. Joy and laughter will creep back in. There is meaning to your days, your actions, and your relationships. You realize what and who is worthy of your attention. Otherwise, time is lost forever. Every chance to make a difference is gone if you're not making the best of every circumstance, including loss.

I can boldly say that every person's purpose is to love others. Why not start there if you are unsure where to find a purpose? There is always meaning in loving others. Without love, life has no meaning. Anyone can find their purpose and meaning in life. How you do it is up to you. This is where you gather the talents you possess and use them

## Chapter 11

to show love toward others. If it's cooking, cook for others. If, like me, it's organizing, help someone get their desk, papers, or other rooms in order. Maybe it's fixing what's broken. For me, it's many things. However, listening and taking the time to make someone feel important is one of my most important gifts. I give to make others feel loved. In return, I feel the joy and peace of living my purpose and finding meaning in life. What is your gift to give?

I learned through my losses that time can be very limited. Therefore, I must be aware of how and who I spend time with. Your relationships are your life. Don't waste time on useless endeavors. I will show you in this chapter and the next how to cultivate them. You have learned skills to deal with all your emotions. You have learned acceptance and can move ahead to cultivate the relationships that enrich you every day.

Here is how you can use your next twenty-four hours to move towards meaning in your relationships. This is a good place to start as you reconstruct your life.

*We each have twenty-four hours each day to do as we choose with whomever we choose. We all have the time. Simply decide what to do with whom in those twenty-four hours. I spent most of my time with Paddy. However, I learned to look upon those I want to spend time with in a calculating way. That sounds harsh, but hear me out. If a person makes me feel better after spending time with them, I spend more time with them. If a person leaves me feeling neither good nor bad, I must decide if they are worth my time today. Maybe I have something to offer them, and perhaps they fill a void of companionship. Then I take the time to do something with them. However, there are people who rain on your every parade with negativity, gossip, and sour grapes. I choose not to chum around with these types or, at the very least, limit time in their presence. I have also learned through my loss and grief journey who my real friends were and who are only with me for selfish reasons. We are all in someone else's company because of what they bring to our lives, as I indicated before. Some people have nothing to give you and only take what you offer. Relationships are a two-way street. There is giving and receiving. It does not have to be an equal giving and receiving. Don't keep count. However, there should be some balance.*

*Paddy taught me to choose my relationships wisely early in my life with him. When Paddy was merely a pupster, I would walk him down the esplanade around our boat, where we lived aboard. Since he was so little still, we would sit and rest periodically. As others would pass by, Paddy would either growl or wag his tail. It was funny to see his discerning tastes. I respected his judgment and have since been alert to who I spend time with. Time is short on this earth, no matter how long it is. Who do you hang with the most? Choose the right atmosphere of positive people who love you and want the best for you. Do they add to your life or steal your joy? Stay away from gossip, strife, and negativity. You will find no joy there.*

Most people seemed to evaluate many things in their life worthy of their time during the pandemic. It was a natural transition to spend time with the most important people who brought the most joy during this time of restriction. Look at what was important to you then and apply it to your life after loss.

This next part of my journal takes you through the grieving process that occurred when we endured the Covid-19 pandemic. I guide you through every stage and what the world was experiencing. See if you relate to this process. It takes one example of loss and applies it to the grieving process.

*Last Journal Entry: Easter 2020*

*I rise early to watch the sunrise. It is Easter, and there will be no celebration, sunrise services, Easter egg hunts, or gathering with lavish lunches of ham and potato salad, Easter eggs, and chocolate bunnies. Our country, our state, is on lockdown. We stay home to protect ourselves from Covid-19, and to protect others from the spread of the virus. We are to go nowhere, unnecessary. Much of the country's work has ceased. We are home alone.*

*It hit me that the entire country was entering the stages of grief. We were grieving the loss of normalcy of work, relationships, and play. I watched as many people went through grief stages as they realized the enormity of the infection and the danger affecting many lives. Most politicians and doctors alike downplayed the severity of the virus when it first hit China. However, we soon saw other countries contracting the flu, and it was on its way to America, where I live.*

*When we were first ordered to stay home, we were in disbelief and* **denial** *that the problem was as big as the media was making it out to be. Denial hit people like a kid caught with their hand in the cookie jar. There was a virus, but I won't catch it, they said to themselves. It's so far away. It has nothing to do with me. But indeed, it had arrived at our doorstep. As information began coming in, most were fearing the worst. This quarantine, or lockdown, was a life unlike any of us had ever known. We were to stay six feet from each other, with no contact, no hugging, just social distancing, no work, church, concerts, or athletic events. Even our parks* were closed. The rules of engagement had changed. We were at a loss of what to do and not do except stay home. Everything was closing down. We couldn't go to work, and we couldn't believe it. Once we realized this quarantine situation was not going away, denial moved aside to let in other emotions.

**Anger** became the first recognizable emotion. We went to the store, and someone was guarding the paper products so we wouldn't grab more than our share. It was apparent others had hogged more than enough to stockpile, leaving little for others. Masks and six-foot distances between each other became the norm. We were all incredulous. We realized this was not going away in two short weeks. Where would we find our money? How were we to pay our bills? Our kids couldn't go to school or play with their friends. How were you going to teach them? Schooling was someone else's job. You had your job. You were mad at China, the government, the fighting politicians, and the people who bought up all the toilet paper! The entire world was in a pickle. The anger you felt was a cover-up to more profound emotions. People lived in fear, uncertainty, and pain. We did not know what was coming. We may have felt deep sorrow over losing jobs, companionship, recreation, and all things familiar. The anger was a mask hiding the pain from this catastrophe. Anger masked a root of bitterness and resentment at life so hard, so unfair. Perhaps your life was hanging by a thread, and this was too much to handle. Or life was a song well sung, a melody in tune, just where you wanted it, but now it was a hodgepodge of uncertainty. There was much to be angry over.

When people were tired of being mad at everyone and everything, they moved to the next stage of grief, **bargaining**. If we could get outside but stay away from everyone, we'd be okay. Sup-

*pose we go to the park and allow the kids to let off steam? If only this is not as bad as they say. I will live a more gracious life, giving what it has blessed me with. I would love to see those I miss so much now. If I could return to work, I'd be on time. Heck, I'd be early if I could go back to my job.* You want life returned to normal. All the deliberations and "What ifs" will not change what's happening. Bargaining only prolongs the inevitable, dealing with a permanently changed life. Our lives will never be the same.

When people realized life would forever change, it sent many over the waterfall of **depression**. As I write this, many are becoming depressed. People are sleeping in, eating and drinking more, and staying in their jammies all day. There are daytime jammies and nighttime jammies. There is an increase in domestic violence and drug use. Suicides are on the rise. We have already scrubbed and cleaned every surface. Many are at a loss for what's next. The children are screaming. They need to play and see their comrades. We all long to see our friends, our grandchildren, and our family. It might even be nice to see coworkers we once enjoyed. The whole scenario is unimaginable and frightening. It's like the sci-fi movie, "The day the earth stood still." We go on living, but don't know why. What's the purpose? In the depressed stage, we felt the depth of the pain. We encounter a place deep within our souls we never knew was there. We may cry as if we will never stop. Cry if you feel tears welling in your eyes. Cry till you can't cry anymore. You will feel better, not worse. Then find the strength you never knew you had to go on.

When you have cried an ocean of tears, you will find some **acceptance** of your present situation. Some things you can't change. Though there are things you can change. Change the things you can and accept what you can't. I see families out hiking. I hear *of a few friends gathering to bike or eat. People spread out in the park. Others accepted that though Covid-19 is still here, they can do things differently. We wear our masks and go out, anyway. We have lost our lifestyles, churches to worship, places to attend fun and exciting events, establishments to meet and eat with friends, and jobs. As time goes on, we see not just what we lost but what we can do about it to go on living. Every morning, we wake up. We learn to live with the loss and the changes. There are those we love in our lives, and we can love them in new and inventive ways. We get creative and life goes on sunset after sunrise.*

*As you make alterations to your lifestyle, you find **meaning and purpose in your life** again. Nothing is the same as before Covid. If you lost a loved one, there is much to love about your life if you seek it. You can't love part of your life. Embrace it all. Every season is part of a whole, your whole life. Adversity can color the lenses through which you look at your world. You have the choice to become bitter over tragedies or stronger. Which will you choose? Learn to enjoy all parts of your life. Seek after joy. It will strengthen you to go on. Joy is the gas to move the car of your life. Eventually, peace follows acceptance. Be content with all you still have. When gratitude fills your heart, you find the purpose and meaning to all that transpired. Your life looks different, but change is good for the soul.*

There are many things to find meaning in your life again. You may even decide to prepare for your death. There is a purpose in taking care of business. You can do what you've always wanted to do and give more back using your talents. Think about telling those you care about, you love them. Do it before it is too late, granting more of yourself than ever before. You can find a purpose beyond your grief. I found some on this website to get you started if you get stuck. However, you can never go wrong with loving others as your purpose.

https://www.lifehack.org/articles/communication/how-put-meaning-back-into-your-life.html

1. Find your purpose

This will give your life meaning. It is why you get up every morning and keep going all day. Your purpose lives in your heart and heals your soul. If loving others is your sole purpose in life, you will have a rich life indeed!

2. Discover your talents

When you follow your talents, you will discover your purpose. If you haven't found what you're good at, ask yourself what comes naturally to you. When you feel at your best, what might you be doing? In what way can you use your talents to help others?

3. Help others

Helping others makes you feel good. You can use your gifts to help those without your talents. Or you can give money, time, or give of yourself in some meaningful way. If you are in the dumps, do something for someone. You won't be feeling down when you have finished helping another.

4. Make personal connections

When you lift others up and share yourself, you can't help but make personal connections and great friends. Don't waste time with people who don't reciprocate or who make you feel worse after being around them.

5. Learn to be happy

If you did the first four steps, you are on the road to happiness. Just remember, no matter what happens, it is your response to your circumstances that makes the difference. If you can't control it, you might as well stay calm and get your happiness on! I learned there are few reasons to get upset.

6. Have a plan

When you have a plan to reach your goals, you have a reason to get up and get going every day. Your plan doesn't have to be earth-shattering. It needs to be something you desire to see in your life. Learn a new skill or something you want to accomplish. Feel a sense of accomplishment when you plan and see it through. Self-fulfillment comes through accomplishment.

7. Do something different

When you have a plan, you put thought into it. Doing something different will take a little thought or it may arise spontaneously. Intentionally go somewhere different to eat. Go to some event, museum, or arboretum you have never seen before. Surprise a friend you haven't seen in a long while with a visit. You can warn them so they are ready. Driving home from work or the store a different way can bring new discoveries. Break from normalcy and shake things up a bit!

8. Turn off your TV

Turning off your TV. may also be living outside your norm. Give yourself a break from the news or your regular programs. Turn it off for a week, a month, all summer, or forever. We can get hooked on shows that don't add to our life. Rather, those constant shows may be taking away from life. TV can be addictive and negative. You will find time for other pursuits. You may find you are happier without TV.

9. Do something you've always wanted to do

You can pursue something that makes you happy now that you are not spending time on mindless TV programs being entertained. There may be something in the back of your mind that pops up occasionally you've always thought about doing. Is there any better time than now? Start a plan to achieve what is in some corner of your mind. Bring it to the forefront.

10. Challenge yourself

When you challenge yourself in some way you take the focus off your problems and focus on something important to you. You have gone through some hard times. Why would I say go challenge yourself? Hard times stimulate growth and strength. Overcoming obstacles builds resilience. When you chose a challenge you are exercising the strength you gained through adversity. Knowing you can overcome obstacles gives you the inner fortitude and motivation to proceed. Chose a small one or a more difficult challenge. It will depend on your personality which way you go. Conquering adversity sets you up for further success that can impact your happiness, health and give you a reason to go on.

You may find other ways to find meaning in your life. I have only given you food for thought. Heartbreak will educate you. It can guide you in living the remaining portion of your lives in joy and zest. You know what and who is important in your life. New knowledge guides you in making decisions that change your life. Most of what you learned is to appreciate time with friends, family, and pets while you still have them. Your journey has revealed a lot about yourself. You know what's important and worthy of your time. You found purpose and meaning, or at least understand what it is and how to achieve balance.

When you have accepted the reality of your loss, you instead focus on searching for your purpose. I have given you many ways to use your purpose in life to find meaning in your days. I have also given you the example of Covid-19 and how our world went through the stages of grief. This example ties together everything I have presented. It gives you a visual of how the process of grief might progress.

Your understanding of emotions and how to negotiate them will strengthen relationships. You know how to express those feelings instead of locking them inside. Your relationships will flourish. When you recognize who you want to spend your time with and appreciate, you feel gratitude and love. In the next and final chapter, I will teach you how to appreciate your loved ones and how to tell them. This may be a turning point from grief to joy. You can find much joy and peace in expressing love to others. Joy because it feels good to show love. Peace because you can live with no regrets. I reveal a technique I have used for years in showing appreciation for those I love. I think you will love it! You will plant and sow seeds of love.

*"More grows in the garden than the gardener knows he has planted."* ~Spanish proverb~

## Points to consider:

- Life has a purpose beyond comfort, joy, and acceptance.
- You have grown during your grief journey and you feel edged on to more meaning to your life.
- Now you can evaluate what is important to you and how to spend the rest of your life.

## Stage Six — Finding meaning in life again
Characteristics:

- A distinct feeling that time is short
- Feeling there is more to life than before your loss
- Being unsure of your purpose
- Thinking more of people than things

Possible actions to take:

- Learn to love others
- Give through your talents to others. Volunteer.
- Consider what your time is worth and use it wisely.
- Choose how and with whom you will spend your time.
- Make goals, have a plan, and work your plan.
- Do something different. Do something you've always wanted to do.
- Turn off your television and social media for a time.
- Give yourself a challenge.

Questions to ponder:

- How can I give back to the world around me?
- How are your relationships?

~~~

*"Don't cry because it's over; smile because it happened."*
*–Theodor Geisel (Dr. Seuss)~*

# CHAPTER 12
# What I Love About You

Live with no regrets about how you have lived and loved, mostly how you have loved. I believe love is all we take with us when we die. And love is the most important thing as we live. There are no safe investments in love. Love comes with risk. However, I would rather live a risky life than a safe life if it means love surrounds me!

When we accept that life will hold some loss and pain, we can further our thoughts on why we find suffering in loss. It is loving them and then losing them that causes the torment. Taking a step back to see what we find painful, we realize love has brought us so much joy, even when it ends in pain. It behooves us to put time into one of the biggest parts of life we take with us when we die, love. If this is not your belief, love is still the most important part of living. No one can take from us the most joyful, free thing on the planet.

Many years ago, I decided I would tell my friends and family what I think about them to their faces while they were still alive. It seemed ridiculous to say nice things about someone at their funeral or memorial. I want them to know while they are alive to bask in my love and adoration. I term this my "living eulogy." It's also called "What I love about you."

I have been doing my "living eulogies" for years and many of my friends and family have received one. I am relieved, I took the time to tell Danny what I loved about him before he passed. Live with no regrets for the people in your life when they pass. Please don't wait another day when you can tell someone you love them, and tell them why. I have told many exactly what I think of them. However, I have many more to write and recite. My journal describes my thoughts on the subject.

*I had been talking about Paddy with someone who knew him and loves him. We both realize the sad past of not having done what we thought we could for a deceased person. Later, after losing that person, we live with the regrets of not saying what we felt, not fully jumping in, no restraints. Our pets don't do that. They are always all in with four paws. Why do we humans restrain ourselves from jumping all in? Why are we so afraid of saying or doing what we feel? I have been in love and have not said so. Who needs to say it first? Who cares who says it first? Who cares who does what first? How silly we humans are not to do what we feel or say how we feel. Why is there fear of the other, not reciprocating, not feeling the same way? If we all said what we think when we feel love, and it was not a bad thing but made someone feel good and loved, wouldn't we have made a difference to someone? What if we all do what our pets do? What if we all let those we love know we love them?*

*If in our pain we blame God or anyone else for it, we can never take steps to heal. God always does His part in transforming life. However, He won't do everything for us. He leads, and we follow. God calls us to act. He also calls us to take the steps of change.*

*Perhaps God is leading me to where He wants me to be, where I can't see. I felt strongly at the beginning of this year that things would change and be different. I felt a transformation was coming into my life. Paddy leaving me was part of that change. Writing about him has given me some comfort, but I know more is coming. As I write this, I realize that perhaps what I have written may also bring comfort to others who are hurting over losing their pet or loved one.*

*Some who have read my simple journal have relayed that I have put into words what they could not. They may have run away in their grief and pain and sought solace in unhealthy ways or a new pet. Many people don't know how they feel or what they feel. They hide their pain and pretend they are fine, going on in their lives as if nothing is disturbing them or disrupting their emotional health. It embarrasses them to be mourning a pet.*

*Some think it's "just a pet." Why do we grieve as though the pet is human? You just get another pet, right? Surely that will take your mind off the death of your beloved pet. Some people don't realize what a pet owner puts into a pet. Non-pet owners don't know their comfort, loyalty, trustworthiness, and love. They don't understand how we can love a pet, a dog like we love our own family. They are just not the same, right? Humans and pets are not the same. It does not mean we can't love them as a family member and mourn their loss as we would the loss of a human. I heard it said by my wise friend Sebastian that our pets and people we love become like artists who die; their artwork becomes more prized after they pass on. Do we not see those we love as more valuable once they are no longer with us? Don't we wish we had told them we love them more often, spent more time with them, cleared up any confusion or rifts, and had more heart-to-heart talks?*

Even though our pets don't tell us they love us, they show us. They make their love very clear. We are the first thing on their mind upon waking in the morning, that is, after potty and food. They know our friends. They know who we don't like, and they don't like them either. Our pets know who we should not like. They know our moods when we are ready to play or just want to be left alone. If we are crying, they are sad, too, so empathetic! They always know when you are coming home before you enter that door. They are waiting with anticipation. Most of us wish for someone to know us so well, not judge us, and then love the bejeebers out of us, anyway. Wouldn't you? Let the ones you love know how much you love them by telling them, "What I love about you," before losing them.

Humans differ greatly from dogs. We have language skills. Most parents show their children how to tell someone they love them. Others may be at a loss for those words that sound so appropriate when someone else says them. All humans crave love, understanding, and comfort. Most crave words of affection and endearment. We all long for someone to say, "I love you." We are not fully living if we do not tell those we love why and how much we love them. What are we holding on to that prevents us from telling those we care about how much we love them? Why are you waiting? Love is the responsibility of allowing it in when appropriate and giving it away. Love is not always easy, but essential to our well-being and very existence. If you decide to love and allow love today, you will never regret that decision. The next step is telling them you love them before it is too late.

## How to write, "What I love about you."

After I decide it's time to tell someone what I love about them, I think about that person for days. I cannot dwell on anything that annoys or bugs me about that person, only positive traits. I start a piece of paper with, "What I love about you" and then their name. Then I list adjectives, behavior, and traits I love about them, unique things, something we shared, and maybe how they affect me. Mostly, I contemplate what I love about who they are as humans on this earth. I will write for days making the words into semi and full sentences. Some people I can write about in one day, in one sitting. Some people take longer. Maybe we had a complex relationship or problems in the past. Some people I could write pages on, but my limit is one page for practical purposes. Every person gets my full consideration and attention. I love to dwell on memories and the person's character. Everyone in my life is unique and special and has affected me differently. Each person deserves my full attention.

Here is an example of overlooking certain character traits. This part can be difficult, but it's how we can love more fully. No person or pet is perfect. We all have character flaws. We are all on our journeys of growth and maturity.

*Yesterday my friend Sebastian came by to bring me some stove-warming wood. Paddy would have greeted him readily. They were terrific friends. I went to welcome my friend instead. Our conversation always gravitates towards Paddy, and it did this time as well. We both miss him so much. Even though Paddy chose me, he would give special people his attention. Sebastian was his surrogate dad. We called him the stepdad. Paddy loved Sebastian, and Sebastian loved Paddy. However, Sebastian hated the doggy hairs that stuck to all things. Somehow, over the years, he overlooked that aspect of Paddy and dealt with it. Many times, he would don Paddy in one of his oversized tee-shirts to keep the hair off him, but eventually, I think he endured the hair just as I did. Just as our friends annoy us in some ways, we look beyond those character traits we dislike and look to the ones that attract us to our friends. Instead, we become grateful for all they are to us. If we didn't ignore some things about our friends, we would go bonkers.*

## Chapter 12

*Sebastian holding Paddy*

*The thing I had to overlook in Paddy was his presence forever underfoot, me tripping over him repeatedly. I would love now to be forever tripping over him. A friend used to complain about her husband, always dropping his clothes wherever he took them off. I asked her if she wouldn't miss those clothes once he was gone. She never complained again. Some things are just not that important.*

This journal entry displays my progress in accepting the things I consider undesirable and looking at the positive.

*I still wake up crying sometimes. I sometimes cry and don't know why. Then I realize I am missing Paddy, and the sadness has surfaced. It still lurks beneath the surface of business and thoughts, but the sadness is there. I have had a friend's dog on loan for a week—my mission is to slim her down and teach her some manners. I trained Paddy in consideration and not to eat what was not his. This dog, Callie, eats everything she can get her teeth into and barks at everything that moves. I have found many things in her bed that didn't belong to her, and she is puking up something she should not have eaten. Ugh. How can you compare a dog without training with the one you had all its life and trained to live a considerate life? Well, you can't. Your dog will always be the winner. She goes home today. I am sad, but I am more sorry that Paddy is not here with me. Callie going home just amplifies that I live alone again. There will be no clicking of toenails on the floor, no thud of a body dropping, no fuzzy creature in my way as I go about my chores, no one begging to go out the door, no barking, just silence as I go about my day. I can hardly stand the quiet sometimes. Don't we get annoyed at their demands? Don't we want to be annoyed again after they've gone?*

*Today, I appreciate how Paddy kept my floor so darn clean, especially on the kitchen floor. Hoover Paddy. He didn't miss a morsel. He would systematically go around the edges and scan for edible scraps of food. Then he would scan around the couch. He was like one of those robot vacuums skimming each inch of the floor, bumping into everything in its way, then turning in another direction. I do so miss my clean floor and Paddy doing his chores. It's nice when your friend's pets visit and clean up the floor, taking over where your pet took off. They know how to get the job done.*

The next step on how to write, "What I love about you."

After thinking of this person for several days, I rearrange the words and semi-sentences into a flow and continuity. I am now ready to fit it on festive stationery they can mount and cherish. I have found many of my "works of art" framed in recipients' homes.

## Reciting "What I love about you."

Next comes the most challenging part for me and the most emotional. I was rarely told "I love you" during my growing-up years, and those words became guarded by my mouth, not easily escaping. To tell someone I love them is a monumental undertaking for me. To make the task harder, I mostly planned to recite my poem in the company of the recipient's friends and family. I not only wanted my special person to know I cared about them and why, but I desired their friends to know they deserved the tribute. I have read my poem before crowds, but the stage still makes me emotional and nervous. That reciting is so difficult for me is more of a testimony to that person I care about. I am doing what is hard for me because they are so special. I have at one time recited "what I love about you" to a whole family. That was nerve-wracking!

I wrote a "What I Love About You" to Paddy and my fiancé, Danny, so you could see what it looks like. I'm so happy and relieved that I told Danny what I loved about him on his birthday only four months before he passed away.

## **What I love about you, Paddy**

With you, I knew secret comfort and a private peace.
There is nothing of value to give me but your love and companionship,
Your unabiding faith in me.
I love that you gave it to the end of time.
Your dark Irish eyes looked deep into my soul.
You saw who I was and loved me, anyway
with unmerited favor and grace.
You tolerated my desires. They were not yours.
Loyal to me and only me.
I love your independence, your strength,
and your stubbornness
That saved you many times in our wilderness.
I loved that you were courageous,
Tackling all things large and small.
You were always there for me
Maybe underfoot, but always present
Waiting for me to arrive, play, or cuddle.
You knew you weren't a dog, but you knew who you were
A big dog in a little body
Oops, did I say "dog" again?
It was as though you were human,
one who loved unconditionally.
You were funny without trying.
I loved that you were smart, so smart.
You were just you,
Whom I loved with all my heart
All these things I love about you, Paddy.

## Chapter 12

## What I Love About You Danny

*A dreamer of a better life, more life*
*A likable guy but*
*Fearless as the lion in the den, ready to stand up to anyone and anything*
*Your faith protecting you always*
*Droll, witty, and fun*
*Loving, kind, and caring*
*Giving and generous, beyond all expectations*
*Always looking for someone to help on their journey*
*Love for the travelers through your life*
*I love that you become wiser, stronger, every day*
*The leader we all look to*
*I even love the "sky is falling you," the frantic "what do I do now?"*
*The answer is always in your heart, even as you ask me.*
*Open to suggestion but non-conforming*
*A hustler at heart for a way of life*
*A growing person within yourself, successful growth*
*On your journey to truth.*
*Soulful as the blues, loving deeply*
*Yearning for all good things*
*Deserving of all good things, of love and truth*
*I love that you are truthful, but not hurtful*
*Soft as a bunny, strong as an ox*
*You value love, friendships, and family.*
*But most of all, I love it when you smile!*
*All these things I love about you.*

It is beneficial to be grateful for what your pet or people taught you. Consider all the time you shared. You will learn to turn gratefulness into communication with those in your life. Tell those you love why you love them. Overlook any character defects. These are the lessons of loving unconditionally. Of course, we will never love unconditionally as a dog does. We all want love in return. It is in loving, regardless of imperfections, that we find meaning in our lives after loss and the process of pain. You are, in essence, turning pain into love again. There are no chains that bind your spiritual self if you take the freedom and time to cultivate all that is within you.

Points to consider:

- Live with no regrets.
- Love is risky but the most important thing we have in this life.
- Anyone can find love. But first you have to be loving.
- It is important to tell those we love that we love them, but we must also tell them why.
- Love is not always easy, but essential to living abundantly.
- When we proceed with a "What I love about you," you begin to look at people differently, more from a positive point of view.

*"The world would be a nicer place if everyone had the ability to love as unconditionally as a dog."~M.K. Clinton~*

*"A dog is the only thing on earth that loves you more than you love yourself." ~Josh Billings ~*

# Conclusion
## The end is never the ending

One of my last journal entries sums up how we don't have to understand everything that happens to us on earth because when we look past adversity, we can see the most important thing to focus on is love. If we live with that in mind, we will have more enriching and loving encounters than difficulties. Life is simpler than we make it sometimes.

*I took Mitch Albom's book, "The Five People you meet in heaven" on vacation with me. It is an enchanting story of one man's life and how it all comes together after he dies trying to save a little girl from certain death. It's Mitch's view of how we will be received in heaven and the people we will meet. Those people tell us how we affected their life. It is neither good nor bad, our fault or anyone else's. It just is. There is the magic of finally understanding what we don't see here on earth. There is a veil that has covered our eyes, now revealing the unseen connection. It is the puzzle pieces falling into place, exposing the complete picture. There will* always be people who affect us in life, and we never realize how much until we reach heaven or the end of our days. I look forward to the day when it all makes sense. Don't you?

I still ponder and wonder why Danny died before we could marry. We had worked out so many things and we had done everything right. I was ready to marry after eighteen long years of being single. He had learned so much about relationships. I learned much about loving imperfectly. We belonged together. I might never understand why we never got to have our glory day, the day we looked deep into each other's eyes and souls and shared our vows. There is a missing piece of the puzzle. We have to go on without understanding.

*Read Mitch's book. His book puts your life in perspective simply, in a way anyone can understand; even if his heaven is not your perspective, it makes sense we will influence many people in our lifetime. Make the most of each chance to make someone grateful to know you. Tell them how thankful you are they are your friend and appreciate what they do for you, no matter how small. Never overlook gratefulness towards how someone smiles at you, dresses nicely to please your eye, or even moves aside in line to let you ahead. Living in peace will open your eyes to many things you never noticed before. Your life will be abundant with things of this world that have nothing to do with possessions, positions, or pride. Peace is a matter of perspective. Peace is gratefulness for what you have and what you have had. I'm not saying there won't be pain in your losses, only that you can be grateful to have known pain. Knowing pain is also knowing joy. It will follow pain. When you feel any emotion, you are living. Be thankful for that.*

*In the meantime, living peacefully does not mean we live a trouble-free life. We may experience fears, make mistakes, say wrong things, and not always be where required when needed. However, peace is still obtainable. With each step we take away from the world's anxiety and worries, we walk towards a peace that surpasses all understanding. There are plenty of circumstances to feel unrest and uncertainty. However, when you live gratefully for all things, you see you are not the one in control. You cannot control what others do, those who leave, or those who die. When someone such as a pet or loved one leaves you by walking out that door or takes one last look at you, you can be thankful they came into your life instead of bemoaning your loss. Even though your loved one may not be here anymore, they arrived. They gave you something to be thankful for, and a sense of peace falls over you that you won't comprehend. We will never understand all things in this lifetime. Why beat yourself up trying to understand them?*

I am sure you understand a lot more about your losses than you did before. Though there are things you still do not understand. You learned many things through life with your pet. My hope here is that you have absorbed the process. I set forth to show you how to grieve a pet loss or any loss in your life. It is a framework from which to identify emotions you perceive. When you make sense of the pain, you can deal with it. If you read my book again after you implement some of my suggestions, you will stumble across more ideas you missed or didn't understand the first time. Your understanding will be more complete the second time. I went through some of my grief books and workbooks several times to gain more understanding.

Part of what Paddy taught me through his death was how to live. We achieve this by going through the grieving process and by recognizing the stages of grief. Knowing where we are on the continuum, we can better understand how to handle it and where we are going on the journey. Grieving is the vehicle in which we recover from our losses and learn life lessons. If you have done the work I set forth, your road to recovery will bring some joy and peace back into your life. You may even find more joy further down the road because you understand yourself, relationships, love, and death better. Life is a self-improvement program that changes and grows you if you allow it. It is change that strengthens you. Making the changes necessary turns uncertainties into courage. You are more able to handle challenges that you might have dreaded previously. Death and loss are always part of your growth but are also useful to others. Everything in your life is not all about you, but always involves others.

Loss is one of the most difficult circumstances we will encounter in life. It is also one of the most transforming experiences. Grief can groom you for your purpose and usefulness to the world. However, it is a bumpy road with many roadblocks. It forces you to slow down and get through tough emotions and things you will never understand. Don't get out of your situation prematurely. Work through the painful process to arrive at a well-developed character and emotional and spiritual maturity. Harvest follows a seed planted. Cultivated over time, you will harvest the growth. You may feel lost many times on your journey, but your GPS will recalculate and set you on your path again. Be patient. Don't give up.

Let's go over some things you should know at this point in your transformation.

# Conclusion

In chapter one, you learned pets come into your home and become family members you fully love and who love you unconditionally. They are the family you choose. No pet is perfect, just as those we associate with are not perfect. However, they can make you laugh with their looks and their antics. They are your constant companions. Pets serve a purpose, just as those in your life serve a purpose. But death always follows life, love, and antics.

Saying goodbye is not what you think about when you take your pet into your home and heart, but in reality, you will lose them someday, and grieving will begin. One thing you may never have contemplated was where one goes after one dies. In chapter two, I emphasize the importance of knowing what you believe about this issue. It is important to take the time to mull over important subjects that may seem meaningless right now, or at least were before your loved one died. If you want to be comforted in another's death, you must determine where you believe they go when they die and when you die. Comfort and peace will result from settling important issues in one's life.

I also cover religion and spirituality in the Life and Death chapter and how they relate to the meaning of life. Knowing what these terms mean to you will carry you a long way on your journey. Whatever your religion, you will still need to know what you value and how you plan to cultivate your spirituality. It will be a personal quest for connection and enlightenment in your world. These are foundational issues concerning life and death. We cannot ignore knowing what these mean and how they shape your life if you seek peace and recovery. Once you go through recovery and arrive at acceptance, there will be a void needing to be filled. You learn how to fill that void as you advance through the chapters to find your purpose and meaning in life. There is nothing mystical about finding one's purpose or meaning to life, though there are many books written on the subject. It can be more simple than you believe. It can simply be loving others.

You will need to become an emotional expert on your journey to recovery. Once you have settled these issues into your soul, you will understand the feelings of joy and peace as they seep in through the cracks of recovery. There was little joy or peace at the beginning of your journey, only pieces of yourself scattered about in disarray. Brokenness is our opportunity to observe our lack of wholeness and spiritual maturity and respond. It is important to understand some key terms, so we are speaking the same language. I wanted you to understand or think about what recovery, joy, and peace mean to you. You can look forward to these results of recovery. They are active endeavors, something you must seek. I hope you got a glimpse of what I am talking about and have caught a joyful or peaceful moment already. The goal of adversity is to give life depth and value, not break you and leave you there. Adversity enlarges your purpose in life and equips you for usefulness. There is a purpose to your pain. However, if you don't change, life won't change. The world owes you nothing. You alone are responsible for your happiness. That realization develops emotional maturity.

You learned about the different stages of grief and what you may go through in response to your loss in the fifth chapter. You may encounter denial, anger, bargaining for a better deal, and a crash with depression you thought would kill you. As you travel that road, you may come to the stop signs of acceptance and wonder about your purpose and future. However, it is this journey that transforms you into someone you weren't before you started. You arrive after the journey, not complete, but more grateful and compassionate. You understand that without love, your life holds no meaning or purpose. If you slowed down long enough, you learned a great deal about life, about what is important and what is not. Losing my pet taught me many life lessons. Losing my fiancé continued to teach me about life and loss. One added to the other.

In chapters six and seven, you learned in the initial grieving that denial and anger might be the first reactions to losing your pet or loved one. You arrive home, and they are gone, but their belongings are still in their place. There is shock and disbelief. There is also so much pain, perhaps turning to anger, at the entire world, at your pet, and even at God. These reactions are entirely normal. Grief is more than pain and shows in many faces. There are usually many underlying emotions beneath anger. I have shown you how to go through and use your anger to discover more about what is beneath, but also about yourself. Anger will alert you to make needed changes.

You may also live with the unforgiveness of many people, including yourself. You have questions to ask yourself regarding unforgiveness. If you answer "yes," then you need to do some work there too. There can be healing in these initial states. You learned there is room for mercy and forgiveness. It is part of the healing. If you stay in this pit, it will turn to self-pity, and then you can never move beyond the initial stages of grief and grow and mature. Don't move on without dealing with your anger. Find out who you are angry with and write a letter to them, even if they are the ones gone. Write one to yourself if need be and forgive yourself! You will find great relief and much growth in this stage. Emotional maturity is knowing how to deal with your emotions, not blaming others for your emotions or your happiness. It does not matter how you feel. It matters what you do.

You may or may not go through the third stage of bargaining. If you do, you will need to recognize it. In chapter eight, you are in so much pain bargaining is your only hope of survival. Your mind keeps you busy making deals where you can. You distract yourself from reality. Your mind occupies itself with "what if" scenarios to avoid pain, putting off suffering. However, you will find all the "what ifs" will not find a solution, only the truth. This is a place of rest before you continue on your journey. However, you don't have to deal with these stormy emotions alone. Grief and pain take a great deal of emotional energy. Sharing your pain, anger, and frustrations gives you relief, perspective, and serenity. Yes, even serenity. Remember, we find serenity through recognizing our powerlessness and being at peace, changing only what we can.

Each step of the way may be triggers. Anything can be a reminder of the one you lost and trigger unfriendly emotions. These will pop up at unexpected times. For me, it's any dog I see in my daily life. Anything involving engagement and marriage is a trigger to remind me I lost my fiancé. When they arise, you feel like they smacked you alongside the head. I would get upset at birthdays, mother's day, and any milestones that reminded me of our life and celebrations.

Also, there may be secondary losses that will elicit unhappy moments to add to your sorrow. In the midst of your pain, is life. The world continues to spin, the clock to tick. You may lose friends, or other pets, experience financial loss, or a living situation may arise that is uncomfortable. Life may stop for us, but it doesn't stop for the world. You may need to address other issues besides the one that caused you grief in the first place. It may not seem fair and more than you can handle. However, you are getting stronger and your courage encourages you to go on. You will be stronger and more resilient because of it. You are learning to bounce back after adversity.

If you went through the bargaining stage, you will be somewhat rested to tackle what I consider the hardest stage of all—depression. In chapter nine, "The Onset of Depression," you learned that though the first stages of grief were terrible enough, the one you enter next is so oppressive you feel like an elephant is sitting on your chest. In a state of depression, nothing has meaning. Everything is pointless. I think of depression as depressing all feelings. However, in this stage, you know if you don't change how you look at life, you won't want to survive. At least in bargaining, you had hopes of survival. My suggestion and what worked for me was to remember your experiences together. Find comfort in friends and the cards you receive. Ruminate on the good times, the times you laughed, and dwelled in pure love with the pet or one you lost. Second, cry your eyes out. It is therapeutic and refreshing when it's over. Again I say, "take your time." Don't hurry through this stage, even if it is uncomfortable. You must stretch to grow. Getting through will be very healing to your soul.

When you have gone through the worst of the worst, you will accept the reality that your loved one is gone and never coming back. Chapter ten helps you experience life and joy after pain. The stage of "acceptance" knows life will hold some loss and pain. It is because we love, we also feel the loss and so much anguish. Love is risky. However, love makes life worth living. There is still life beyond loss. Edge yourself into the enrichment and deep fulfillment of life. It does us no good to live in the cycle of confused, hopeless, or emotional thought patterns that can damage the soul. Be especially good to yourself. In the acceptance stage, you will be more prone to get out and enjoy something that is good for your body and soul. You have been through tough times. I can hear Danny, my fiancé, say, "Babe, if you want it, buy it. If you want to do it, do it." I try to listen and be good to myself. It feels good. I probably have never been this good to myself.

Acceptance does not mean you want to accept your loved one is gone. It means you see the truth and you can deal with it with strength and courage. Acceptance is acknowledging your mix of emotions and making sense of them. There will be times you recognize and feel a particular emotion but do nothing more. Then, other times, you must feel them and do something about them. Finally, you will find relief and a healthy sense of self and empowerment in acceptance. Previously, you reacted to emotion out of survival. Now you can take a calculated approach. You can use that emotion to make changes beneficial to your well-being. You don't have control over life circumstances. However, you can control your reaction to them. You can find serenity when you accept this principle. When you feel more acceptance than disbelief, you will decide more confidently. Acceptance will not happen all at once, but a little at a time. Though one day you might have the epiphany that you accept your loss. You will feel ready for more. Realize the end of something is better than the beginning. You appreciate something difficult or not just given to you. You worked for every bit of progress you made. Appreciate where you are even if it's not where you will be, eventually. Nothing is free. Any progress you worked for, you did it and you can pat yourself on the back. Celebrate every victory regardless of how small.

Chapter eleven tells you exactly how you can live again by focusing on those still here on this earth for you to love. You can find purpose and meaning in your life beyond your adversity. It means focusing on the important, nonmaterial things of life. These things can easily slip through your fingers when you are busy or doing what you think you ought to do. Grief slows us down to see love, appreciation, gratitude, joy, and peace. No one can take those intangibles from you. Your life has a purpose beyond comfort or pleasure. I supply many ideas on how to find your purpose and, thus, the meaning of life. The most important outcome of adversity is not necessarily joy and peace, but your own character's development. You realize if you go with the flow, you will not grow.

Love is one purpose we can all have. We accept that love is risky business. If we love, we can lose our love object. If we don't love, we lose life. When we live with purpose, we live like there is no tomorrow. It might just be so.

Live with no regrets about how you have lived and loved, mostly how you have loved. Telling someone you love them and why will change their lives and yours forever. When you begin to love again, you find meaning in your life, as I explained in chapter eleven. You are now a different person. You learned through love and death there is more to love and experience. If you are still here on earth, you have a purpose. See what and who is worthy of the time you have left to live. As you maneuver that treacherous road of love, the chains that bound you are broken. You went from broken to broken chains that bind. You are free to love and live. Love is risky, but loving is life.

*"Image living life so carefully, that there are no signs you lived at all."*
*~Raven Leilani, Luster~*

I know you probably went through this book in some emotional state, because of your own painful experience or reading about mine. However, I did not write this book to leave you in a state of emotional pain. I wrote so you have a framework to follow and some solutions to all you experienced, and perhaps prevent some of the turmoil you might go through without guidance. Remember, grief serves the purpose of getting you through the pain and coming out the other side renewed and ready to live life to its fullest. I don't believe that "time heals all wounds". Time may lessen the pain, but you may always feel the pain of loss. My hope is for you to grasp the perspective that life still joyfully holds purpose despite your loss.

You will someday be in a position to help others through their grief. Even knowing you have lost and lived through loss can help give others a long-term perspective. They see perhaps they can do it too. Love and what we learn in our lives are for sharing. However, none of these changes happen instantaneously. Grief takes time, and all you have undergone is normal, normal for you. Be patient. Live your journey out. Most importantly, keep showing up!

It takes more than patience with yourself for this journey. It also takes a great deal of courage and perseverance to face loss and grief. Life will be challenging. The imbalance needs to be stabilized. There are new routines and habits. You will experience imbalances of physical, mental, emotional, and spiritual aspects to your soul. It is a challenge to deal with new feelings, limitations, and advice to endure these trials and keep your perspective. You need to make the necessary changes. It takes strength and courage to be unafraid to take action. Courage will help you make decisions instead of reacting to all the imbalances.

It takes inner fortitude to gain the strength needed to get beyond the pain. You need to get beyond yourself. In all your pain, you might feel you could never accomplish that outcome. You must. Remember when I said self-pity is a pit you will stay in if you don't consciously do something about it? Courage helps you get past pain and frustrations to have concern for others. You have become a better person because of the pain and trials. This is one result of all your hard work on this rough and bumpy road. Doing for others out of love brings more joy and peace than any endeavor in life.

You might feel you have nothing to give someone when you are empty. There is certainly a hole in your soul without your loved one. It will take courage to give when you believe there is nothing to give. However, I have found when you do—you have more after you give than before. Your heart fills with joy, taking the place of sorrow. The process takes an exercise of will backed by strength through courage. You need to hold fast to your newfound strength because there are those who will come against you. Not everyone will be for you, as you assume. Decide how you will respond. Your courage will give you the power. A rational mind when you think through your life issues and concerns will help you stand on what you value. You may have already experienced the joy of giving to others if you have followed my advice. I know you can find strength and courage within yourself if you seek deep within your spirit and soul. It is there for you to find. It all takes time. Sorrow has forced you to take that slow road to relief, giving you time to make changes within yourself. As I have said, this journey takes hard work and time. Take the time to find your courage and new life beyond your wildest dreams.

Maturity puts everything in perspective. You know there will be valley and peak experiences. Knowing this helps you to understand nothing is permanent. If you are a hiker, you know the path is never level or straight. You go into the valley to find water. You climb back up to view the great beyond. It's about learning more in the valleys than the mountaintops. One must embrace change to stretch and grow. You cannot live your life in abundance without change. We do not live life merely getting by. Maturity is living life comfortably in the face of change. Like where you are. Your life is not a burden but a song you sing. Live the life you were given, because there may be no tomorrow. Of that, I am certain.

The overall benefit of my book is finding a way through grief. You will learn how to become grateful and compassionate because of your grief. Life will become full of meaning and rich relationships. My book is about becoming a better person because of trials and pain. It's about becoming stronger and more courageous. Your transformed self will deal with life differently because you are different. You now acknowledge what your pet and others have taught you. Learning how to navigate the grief journey with its twists and turns gets you in touch with the emotions that life amplifies. You will become grateful for even the negative emotions directing you in a way ignoring them never will.

Life is meant to be lived to the fullest, no matter how long that life may be. It's about being the best you can be. Keep showing up. Never give up. Most importantly, live with no regrets for how you have lived and loved, mostly how you have loved. Love is all we take with us when we die and the most important thing while we live. Live it. Share it.

*"Death is not the greatest loss in life, but the beginning of a transformed life." ~Diana Lee~*

~~~

Please feel free to email me about how my book helped you. I began writing for myself. I finished it for you. Together we become better.

Email: dianaleemoran@gmail.com

Email a review for my book on the site where you purchased it so that others can know if they want to read it.

~~~

I have included *The Rainbow Bridge* poem in my book because I love it, and it seems an appropriate way to end my book. After I lost Paddy, I received many versions of the poem. I tweaked them all creating this version. The author is unknown.

## The Rainbow Bridge

*Just this side of heaven lies the Rainbow Bridge*
*When a beloved pet dies, especially close to someone here, it crosses the Rainbow Bridge. It makes friends on the other side with other animals and frolics over rolling hills and peaceful lush meadows of green. The sun is warm, and they are as healthy and playful as we remember them in days gone by. full of the vigor of youth.*

*Together the animals chase and play, content and happy, except for one thing. Each pet misses that person special to them left behind. The day comes when a pet will suddenly stop and look off into the distance… bright eyes intent, eager body quivering, suddenly recognizing you. Your pet leaves his newfound friends and bounds quickly across the green fields and into your embrace. You celebrate in joyous reunion. You will never again separate.*

*Happy tears and kisses are warm and plentiful upon your face. Your hands caress the face you missed. You look deep into the loving and trusting eyes of your pet and know that you never really parted. You realize that though out of sight, your love has been remembered. In a joyful reunion, you cross the Rainbow Bridge together on that long walk into forever…*

*Author unknown but fully acknowledged*

*Paddy at 16 in his last days*

## "To Live in Hearts We Leave Behind is Not to Die"

### ~Thomas Campbell~

~~~

## URGENT PLEA!

### Thank You For Reading My Book!
I really appreciate all of your feedback and
I love hearing what you have to say. If it helps you,
it will help others and together we become better.

.

I need your input to make the next version of this
book and my future books better.

Please take two minutes now to leave a helpful review on
Amazon letting me know what you thought of the book:

Thanks so much!
**Diana Lee Moran**

# Acknowledgments

*Floppy Ears* would not be complete without acknowledging the people who contributed to this endeavor. We can do nothing in life on our own. There are those who birth the idea, as did my friend Tena Clark. The first editor, Shasha Braun tore apart my book and caused me to write a much better book at the rewrite. There were many friends who encouraged me to get through the hard process, as I was grieving all the while writing. People like Ruth Ruiz, Rusty Howe, Kasey Moran, Price Assay, Sheri and Mark Myer, my mom Dixie, Danny Williams, Wilma Rexwinkel, my brother Doc Macomber, and on and on. I could not have endured had it not been for all my friends and family. After the first copy, Michael Foley edited it again and found many redeeming qualities in my book. He encouraged me to continue writing books and so I think I shall! Look for following books in the future.

**Self-Publishing School**

**NOW IT'S YOUR TURN**

**Discover the EXACT 3-step blueprint you need to become a bestselling author in as little as 3 months.**

Self-Publishing School helped me, and now I want them to help you with this FREE resource to begin outlining your book!

Even if you're busy, bad at writing, or don't know where to start, you CAN write a bestseller and build your best life.

With tools and experience across a variety of niches and professions,
Self-Publishing School is the only resource you need to take your book to the finish line!

**DON'T WAIT**

Say "YES" to becoming a bestseller:

**https://self-publishingschool.com/friend/**

Follow the steps on the page to get a FREE resource to get started on your book and unlock a discount to get started with Self-Publishing School

# Index of Quotes

**Introduction**

*"Our pets don't live as long as we do because they already know what it takes us humans so long to learn." ~Diana Lee~*

**Chapter 1 Expert on Grieving?**

*"A loss not grieved is a life half lived." ~Diana Lee~*

*"God works on us as we journey, grow, and learn to live through these life events for which we are never ready." ~Diana Lee~*

**The Day Paddy Died**

*"When we adopt a dog or any pet, we know it is going to end with us having to say goodbye, but we still do it." ~W. Bruce Cameron~*

*"If there are no dogs in Heaven, then when I die, I want to go where they went." ~Will Rogers~*

## Chapter 2 Pet or Friend

*"Before you get a dog, you can't quite imagine what living with one might be like; afterward, you can't imagine living any other way."* ~Caroline Knapp~

*"The world would be a nicer place if everyone had the ability to love as unconditionally as a dog."* ~M.K. Clinton~

*"Dogs are not our whole life, but they make our lives whole."* ~Roger Caras~

## Chapter 3 Life After Death

*"When I look into the eyes of an animal, I don't see an animal. I see a living being. I see a friend. I feel a soul."* ~Anthony Douglas Williams~

*"Death is not the greatest loss of life. The greatest loss is what dies inside us while we live."* ~Norman Cousins~

## Chapter 4 Recovery Joy Peace

*"Recovery is a process. It takes time. It takes patience. It takes everything you got."* ~Diana Lee~

*"We learn more in our valley experiences than on our mountain tops."* ~Charles Stanley~

## CONCLUSION

*"Quit trying to be who you were and try being who you are now."*
*~Diana Lee~*

*"The deeper your sorrow carves into your being, the more joy you can contain." ~Kahlil Gibran~*

*"Every day wasted is a day you will never get back." ~Joyce Meyer~*

*"The only way to get to the other side is through the door." ~Helen Keller~*

### Chapter 5 What are the Stages of Grief?

*"Healing involves discomfort, but refusal to heal is infinitely more painful." ~Diana Lee~*

*"I am certain that learning to recognize and execute emotions will make your world a better place to live." ~Diana Lee~*

*"Don't ask for a blessing—be a blessing." ~Diana Lee~*

### Chapter 6 Stage One Denial

*"Denial is the door she slams in her own face, trapping her in this lonely comfort zone. It keeps her from facing what hurts." ~Judith Sills~*

*"The pit is the beginning of a pity part. Don't stay there." ~Diana Lee~*

*"Compassion opens the door to patience, kindness, generosity, and actions rooted in love." ~Charles Stanley~*

"When you feel dog tired at night, it may be because you growled all day." ~Anonymous~

## Chapter 7 Stage two Anger

"Anger is the calling card no one wants to accept." ~Diana Lee~

"If what we are doing with our anger is not achieving the desired result, it would seem logical to try something different." ~Harriet Lerner~

"If you are patient in one moment of anger, you will escape a hundred days of sorrow." ~Chinese Proverb~

"Anger makes you smaller while forgiveness forces you to grow beyond what you were." ~Cherie Carter Scott~

"Anybody can become angry. That is easy; but to be angry with the right person, and to the right degree, and at the right time, and for the right purpose, and in the right way, that is not within everybody's power, that is not easy." ~Aristotle~

## Chapter 8 Working Through the Grief- Stage three-Bargaining

"Our culture thrives on black-and-white narratives, clearly defined emotions, easy endings, and so, this thrust into complexity, exhausts." ~Caroline Knapp~

"Grief is like the ocean—it comes on waves ebbing and flowing. Sometimes the water is calm, and sometimes it is overwhelming.

*All we can do is learn to swim."* –Vicki Harrison~

## Chapter 9 The Onset of Depression

*"When you adopt a dog, you have a lot of very good days and one very bad day."* -W. Bruce Cameron~

*"What soap is to the body, tears are for the soul."* ~Yiddish proverb~

*"Sometimes memories sneak out of my eyes and roll down my cheeks." From a book called Annie, the truth behind what really happened.~Mark Myer~*

## Chapter 10 Moving on With Our Lives — Acceptance

*"Love knows not its own depth until the hour of separation."* – Kabil Gibran~

*Serenity Prayer*

## Chapter 11 Finding Meaning in Life Again

*"Heartbreak is life educating us."* –George Bernard Shaw~

*"More grows in the garden than the gardener knows he has planted."* ~Spanish proverb~

## Chapter 12 What I Love About You

"Don't cry because it's over—smile because it happened." –Theodor Geisel (Dr. Seuss)~

"The world would be a nicer place if everyone had the ability to love as unconditionally as a dog." ~M.K. Clinton~

## Conclusion The end is never the ending

"A dog is the only thing on earth that loves you more than you love yourself." ~Josh Billings~

"Imagine living life so carefully that there are no signs you lived life at all." ~Raven Leilani, Luster~

"Death is not the greatest loss in life, but the beginning of a transformed life." ~Diana Lee~

## Crossing Over The Rainbow Bridge

"To Live in Hearts We Leave Behind is Not to Die." ~Thomas Campbell ~

Link here to download the Index
https://dl.bookfunnel.com2fxjby4ers

# Index to the Stages of Grief

**Stage 1—Denial**
Characteristics:

- Shock and numbness
- Confusion and disbelief
- Dreamlike state and fear
- Pain
- Survival mode

Possible action to take:

- You can continue to ask yourself the inevitable questions. The answers will bring the denial to the surface so you can face reality.
- You can also surround yourself with those who listen and bring you comfort, without advice or judgment.
- Give yourself time alone to feel your sorrow.
- Don't make any life-altering decisions.

- Get up and get on with your living habits to feel some normalcy.
- Write in your journal. List what you are and aren't in control of.

Question to ask yourself:

- Could you really have prevented their death? Are you in control of anything that happens, such as death? The only thing you can control is your response.

**Stage 2—Anger**
Characteristics:

- Rage
- Hurt, sadness, and loneliness
- Panic, fear, and anxiety
- Resentment
- Guilt
- Powerless
- Uncomfortable in your feelings and acceptance of those feelings
- Unforgiveness

Possible action to take:

- You can wear yourself out crying, a good cleansing cry.
- Or go outside, garden, hike, bike, walk, dance, or do anything that externalizes the agony you feel inside.

Get yourself exhausted.
- Only be around people you feel fully comfortable with who love you, regardless of your behavior or outbursts.
- Take all the comfort offered to you.
- Forgiveness may be in order to get through the anger, forgiveness of the deceased, and others who say or do the wrong things. Forgive yourself. You are not at fault. Get a good book on forgiveness if this is a problem for you.
- Talk to your loved ones and tell them all you want them to know. Write them a letter or write it in your journal so you can go back later and see your progress.
- Write in your journal. List what you are and aren't in control of.

Question to ask yourself:

- What feelings are beneath all that rage?

**Stage 3 — Bargaining**
Characteristics:

- You may feel hopeful and a bit more at rest, but only because you are asking "what if" questions and rationalizing
- Guilt and asking the questions, "What if…"
- Fantasizing different outcomes

- Rationalization
- There may be feelings of uneasiness at all you may feel, usually near the end of the stage

Possible actions to take:

- Look around to those you love and can still love.
- Do not be resistant to any feelings you are experiencing. Let them flow.
- Try to contend with only one emotion at a time.
- Do not get too busy. You still have a way to go.
- Share your feelings of pain, anger, and frustration either with a good listener, grief group, or counselor. A counselor at any stage is therapeutic if you need it.
- Write in your journal.

Questions to ask yourself:

- What will you gain by feeling the pain now? What do you have to lose?
- Is there someone who has lost something, too? How can you help them?

**Stage 4–Depression**
Characteristics:

- Overwhelming sorrow and heaviness
- Hopelessness and despair
- Depleted and empty
- Deflated, no energy for living, overwhelming fatigue

- Loss of interest in the process or joys of life, nothing worth doing
- Feeling life ripped you off, and life is not fair
- Inability to focus
- Inability to sleep or sleep too much

Possible actions to take:

- Allow all the feeling to wash over you
- Ruminate on the fun times when you laughed and felt the love.
- Appreciate the time you had together.
- Cry if you feel like it and don't feel ashamed.
- Laugh too, at the funny things they did or said, and don't feel bad that you laughed.
- Share your stories or write them down.
- Write about all your feelings in a journal.

Questions to ask yourself:

- If it's natural to feel depressed at our loss, why not feel the grief and pain?
- What did you learn about love and life from the one you lost?

**Stage 5 — Acceptance**
Characteristics:

- You may feel more often feelings other than grief.
- You may catch yourself laughing and feeling joy or elation.
- You may see more clearly and look to your future
- You can now make decisions. Don't tackle any life-altering ones just yet, unless life forces it upon you to be financially secure or safe.
- You may still feel uneasiness. Acceptance does not mean you are at total peace over your loss.
- Acceptance reminds you, you are not in control of anything but your own responses.
- You may have a peaceful day, a joyful moment, and feel loved and loving

Possible actions to take:

- Do not compare your grief with anyone else's.
- Have something to believe in.
- Take time for self-care, whatever it is, to pamper yourself.
- Join in where you feel comfortable.
- Play
- Get into some good habits and challenge yourself at something.
- Realize all you have to be grateful for.
- You might also find it helpful to continue with any forgiveness needed.

Questions to ask yourself:

- What have you learned about yourself?
- Who are you now having learned and loved this person or pet?

**Stage 6–Finding meaning in life again**

- A distinct feeling that time is short
- Feeling there is more to life than before your loss
- Being unsure of your purpose
- Thinking more of people than things

Possible actions to take:

- Learn to love others
- Give through your talents to others. Volunteer.
- Consider what your time is worth and use it wisely.
- Choose how and who you spend your time with.
- Make goals, have a plan, and work your plan.
- Do something different. Do something you've always wanted to do.
- Turn off your television and social media for a time
- Give yourself a challenge.

Other Possibilities:

- Look to new perspectives. Listen to those around you. Listen as someone pours their pain out.
- Make choices you are in control of.

- Do something new, meet new people, and make new friends.
- Use all your senses to feel alive again, see every shape, smell deeply the surrounding air, listen to life, feel the textures of everything you touch, from soft to gritty, and eat foods that taste good. Everything may feel new to you now.
- Learn something new; a craft, art, a dance, a language, anything out of your normal realm of interest.
- Go a different way to places you frequent.
- Watch a sunrise. Watch a sunset.
- Read a book that causes you to look at life differently.
- Turn off the TV.
- Rearrange your drawers or living room. Move things around and get rid of old dusty things on shelves.
- Clean out clutter.
- Tell those you love why you love them. Never leave someone without saying, "I love you."
- Choose how and with whom you will spend your time.
- By all means, cry when your pain rises to the surface in all this newness.
- Be grateful for all you have and how much you have loved and been loved this side of heaven. Write a gratitude journal.
- Know we are all in this together. We all have known loss and grief.

Questions to ask yourself:

- How can I give back to the world around me?
- How are my relationships?
- Am I making the most of every day?
- Am I giving to others of my talents and time?
- Am I seeing life through fresh eyes because of what I have endured?

This is not an exhaustive list of characteristics and actions you can take to go through the grieving process. This is a handy index to check on your progress or remind you of ideas to help you progress. Some of the most important things you can do are surround yourself with loved ones but have time alone, too. Write in a journal and see a therapist or join a grief group. Get plenty of rest and get outside. Do something nice for someone else and change your perspective for a moment. Most of all, remember those still living for you to love and find comfort in their presence. When you remember what you have lost, also remember those still living. Take all the time you need with the process. Be gentle with yourself.

What I love about you.

Points to consider:

- Live with no regrets.
- Love is risky but the most important thing we have in this life.

- Anyone can find love. But first you have to be loving.
- It is important to tell those we love that we love them, but we must also tell them why.
- Love is not always easy, but essential to living abundantly.
- When we proceed with a "What I love about you," you begin to look at people differently, more from a positive point of view.

It is the death or loss of someone that causes us to ponder life's biggest questions. Death teaches us how to live and we can learn to live in abundance.

One last question-

How do you plan to live the rest of your life?

~~~

Credit: Child Therapy Toys - Childswork/Childsplay

Made in United States
North Haven, CT
07 November 2024

59975966R00147